MW01503347

The AI Handbook for Everyone

The Ultimate AI Resource for Using ChatGPT, Canva, Ideogram, MidJourney & Dall-e + 100 Prompts!

PJ Chavaux

Copyright © 2025 by PJ Chavaux

All rights reserved.

No portion of this book may be reproduced in any form without written permission from the publisher or author, except as permitted by U.S. copyright law.

Contents

Introduction

Introduction

In a world where technology moves faster than a speeding bullet, AI has become the new superhero on the block. But fear not, dear reader! You don't need to be a tech wizard or a mad scientist to harness the power of AI. In fact, with "The AI Handbook for Everyone," you'll discover that AI is not just for the elite few, but for anyone who wants to make their life a little easier and a lot more fun.

Now, you might be thinking, "AI? Isn't that something only geniuses can understand?" Well, let me tell you a secret: AI is just a fancy way of saying "really smart computer programs." And guess what? You don't need a Ph.D. to use them! This book is here to guide you through the wonderful world of AI, one laugh-out-loud example at a time.

So, what makes "The AI Handbook for Everyone" different from all those other AI books out there? For starters, it's written by someone who knows that life is too short to be serious all the time. As an author with a passion for helping adults, seniors, and parents navigate the sometimes-scary waters of technology, I've made it my mission to make AI accessible to everyone. No jargon, no complicated formulas, just straight-up, easy-to-understand guidance that will have you using AI like a pro in no time.

Inside these pages, you'll find 100 examples of how you can use tools like ChatGPT, Midjourney, Ideogram, Canva, and Dall-e to make your life easier and more fun. From generating business letters to whipping up recipes, these AI tools are like having a personal assistant, a chef, and a creative guru all rolled into one. And the best part? You don't have to pay them a salary!

But this book isn't just about examples. It's also about showing you how AI is already being used in everyday life and small businesses. We'll dive into three case studies that will blow your mind and make you wonder how you ever lived without AI. From a small bakery that uses AI to create custom cake designs to a senior center that uses AI to keep residents engaged and entertained, these real-life stories will inspire you to think outside the box and embrace the possibilities of AI.

Throughout the book, we'll explore key themes and concepts that will help you understand AI in a whole new light. We'll talk about how AI can save you time and money, how it can help you be more creative, and how it can even improve your relationships. Yes, you read that right! AI isn't just about technology; it's about making your life better in every way possible.

Now, I know what you're thinking. "This all sounds great, but what's in it for me?" Well, my friend, let me tell you. Whether you're a student looking to ace your exams, a senior looking to stay sharp, a n office worker looking to impress your boss, or a technician looking to streamline your workflows, this book has something for you. It's the ultimate resource for anyone who wants to use AI to make their life easier, more productive, and more enjoyable.

So, what are you waiting for? Dive in and discover the power of AI for yourself! In the coming chapters, we'll explore each of the key AI tools in depth, with plenty of examples and case studies to keep you entertained and informed. And by the end of the book, you'll be an AI whiz, ready to take on the world one smart computer program at a t ime.

Remember, AI is not something to be feared or avoided. It's a tool that can help you achieve your goals, pursue your passions, and live your best life. So, let's embrace the future together and see where AI can take us. I promise you; it's going to be one heck of a ride!

Chapter One

Demystifying AI for the Everyday User

Remember the first time you used a smartphone and realized it could do more than just make calls? You were probably amazed to discover it could play music, take photos, and even remind you to pick up milk at the grocery store. Fast forward to today, and Artificial Intelligence, or AI, is doing for technology what the smartphone did for communication—making it smarter and more useful in ways you never imagined. But before you start picturing robots taking over your kitchen or your car driving you to work while you nap, let's clear up a few things. AI isn't about creating a world where machines rule; it's about making your life easier, your work more efficient, and your free time more enjoyable. It's about adding a dash of smartness to everyday tasks, like having a personal assistant with a never-ending coffee supply who never needs a break.

AI in Everyday Language: What You Need to Know

Let's get one thing straight: Artificial Intelligence is just a high-tech way of saying "smart technology." It's not some sci-fi fantasy; it's real, and it's here to make your life a little less complicated. Think of AI as that helpful neighbor who knows everyone in the block and seems to have a solution for any problem. Except, this neighbor doesn't borrow your lawnmower or forget to return your casserole dish. AI is about making computers smart enough to perform tasks that usually require human intelligence. It's the brains behind Siri answering your question about the weather, Alexa reminding you of your dentist appointment, and Netflix knowing just what kind of movie you need to unwind after a long day.

But how does this so-called "smart technology" actually work? It's all about learning from examples, or what the tech-savvy folks call machine learning. Imagine teaching a child to recognize a dog. You show them pictures of dogs, point out the similarities and differences, and soon, they can spot a dog from a mile away. AI does the same thing but with a lot more data and a lot less drool. It learns to recognize patterns, make decisions, and even translate languages in real time. It's like having a multilingual friend who never gets tired of helping you out.

Now, you might be wondering, "Is AI going to take over my job?" Rest assured, AI isn't here to replace you; it's here to work alongside you. Picture AI as your trusted sidekick, the Robin to your Batman. In healthcare, AI assists doctors in diagnosing diseases with precision. In design, it acts as a creative partner, suggesting ideas you might not have thought of. It's not about taking over; it's about teaming up to do great things together. So, when you see AI in action, remember it's not a threat—it's an opportunity to make your life better, one smart decision at a time.

Exercise: Spot AI in Your Daily Life

Next time you're watching TV, scrolling through your social media feed, or even just checking your email, take a moment to notice where AI is at work. Is it suggesting a show you might like? Filtering out spam emails? Reminding you of your friend's birthday? Jot down these examples and see just how integrated AI already is in your daily routine. You'll be surprised at how much of your day is quietly optimized by this invisible, yet incredibly helpful technology. By the end of this exercise, you'll have a newfound appreciation for the AI working behind the scenes, making your life just a little bit easier.

Breaking Down the Basics: How AI Works Without the Tech Jargon

Let's sidestep the baffling buzzwords and get straight to the meat and potatoes of AI. Think of AI as a diligent intern who learns by example and never tires. How does this marvel manage to mimic human tasks? At its core, AI operates through a process called machine learning, which is a bit like how a toddler learns to identify animals. You show a toddler pictures of cats and dogs, and eventually, they figure out the difference. AI does this, but on a grander scale, and with more data than you can shake a stick at. It starts with data input, where vast amounts of information—think of it as a buffet of numbers, words, and pictures—are fed into a system. This system then recognizes patterns, much like how you might notice that every time you eat ice cream, you feel a little happier. Through this pattern recognition, AI starts to "understand" its tasks, albeit in a very mechanical way.

Now, calling AI intelligent might be a stretch. It doesn't think or feel, but it sure knows how to follow patterns. Imagine you're teaching a dog new tricks. You reward it with treats every time it gets it right, and over time, it learns what you want it to do. This is similar to how AI processes information through example-based learning. It's like training a pet that never needs a walk or a bath. AI's development has seen stages that mirror the growth of a child. In the early days, it was about basic recognition—identifying a cat from a dog. But as it grew, it learned to make more complex decisions, thanks to something called deep learning. Deep learning is like giving AI a pair of glasses to see the world in high definition. It allows AI to process information in layers, much like how you peel an onion, except without the tears.

The evolution of AI hasn't happened overnight. It took years of research and development to reach our current state. Historically, AI began with simple tasks, like playing chess—running on rules and logic. Over time, it embraced neural networks, which operate a bit like the human brain, processing information in a web of connections. Picture a large spaghetti bowl, where each strand connects to another, passing information along until it reaches a conclusion. This web allows AI to handle complex tasks, from recognizing emotions in a voice to predicting the weather.

When it comes to learning methods, AI has a few tricks up its sleeve. You have supervised learning, where AI is like a student with a tutor, receiving feedback to improve. Then there's unsupervised learning, where it's more like a kid exploring a new playground without a map, figuring things out on its own. Lastly, there's reinforcement learning, a bit like playing a video game where AI sharpens its skills by trial and error, continuously adjusting to score points. These methods highlight AI's ability to adapt and refine its understanding, albeit through a series of rigid rules and calculations.

AI's development and learning processes may sound like a sci-fi narrative, but they're rooted in the everyday logic of trial, error, and adjustment. It's a system that's continuously evolving, striving to mimic our brain's intricate pathways without ever needing a cup of coffee or a nap. AI's journey, from its humble beginnings to its current capabilities, showcases a remarkable trajectory of growth and potential, one that's poised to keep expanding, much like our universe of possibilities.

AI Myths Debunked: Separating Fact from Fiction

In a world teetering on the brink of digital transformation, AI myths abound like a persistent game of whack-a-mole. Just when you think you've squashed one, another pops up. The most cinematic among these tales is the idea that AI will take over the world. Picture a parade of robots marching down Main Street, demanding your Wi-Fi password. Reality check: AI isn't plotting a coup. It lacks ambition, dreams, and the capacity to scheme world domination. AI is a tool, a mighty impressive one, but a tool nonetheless. It's here to help, not overthrow. It follows commands, it doesn't give them, and it certainly doesn't have a sinister agenda tucked away in its code. If it ever did, it would probably just suggest you try a different recipe for banana bread.

Another common misconception is the belief that AI is infallible, akin to a digital deity that never errs. But let's face it, even the most advanced algorithms can't escape a bad day. AI's intelligence is simulated, not genuine. It relies heavily on the data it's fed, which means if you input garbage, you get garbage. It's called garbage in, garbage out.

Like giving a chef spoiled ingredients and expecting a gourmet meal. AI can't intuit or improvise; it follows the data trail laid out before it. So, when it stumbles, it's not the machine's fault but a reflection of flawed data or design. AI doesn't have a mind of its own—it's more like a high-tech paintbrush than an artist.

Then there's the misguided notion that AI can think like a human. As much as we romanticize the idea of machines with minds, AI lacks consciousness. It doesn't daydream, reminisce, or worry about its to-do list. AI processes information through complex algorithms, not thoughts. It's like comparing a calculator to a philosopher. Calculators compute; philosophers ponder the meaning of life. AI can mimic human behavior to a degree, but it doesn't understand it. It can recognize your face in a crowd, sure, but it doesn't ponder why you chose that particular shirt today.

AI's capabilities are vast, but they have boundaries. It leans heavily on human input and data quality. Think of it as a highly efficient car—it can get you from A to B swiftly, but you need to steer. If the data fueling AI is skewed or biased, the results will be too. Human intuition, that gut feeling that tells you not to answer the phone when a telemarketer calls, is something AI can't replicate. It can analyze patterns, but it doesn't have a hunch. AI's strengths lie in processing vast amounts of information quickly, not in making nuanced judgments.

Ethical concerns about AI are valid and worth discussing. Privacy issues, for instance, are a hot topic. When you think about it, AI's voracious appetite for data can be a double-edged sword. While it enables personalized experiences, it also raises questions about data usage and security. Algorithms can harbor biases, reflecting the prejudices of the data they're trained on. It's a bit like inheriting your grandmother's secret recipe—it might need tweaking to suit modern tastes. Yet, AI also holds immense promise. In education, it can tailor learning experiences to individual needs, making learning as unique as the students themselves. In healthcare, AI can analyze patient data to suggest more effective treatments, acting as a valuable assistant to medical professionals.

As we continue to explore AI's potential, it's crucial to approach it with a balanced perspective. AI isn't going to take over, nor is it a flawless oracle. It's a powerful tool that, when used wisely, can transform lives for the better. So, don't fear the bots; understand them. They're here to assist, enhance, and maybe even make you laugh when they misinterpret a command. AI's future is bright, not because it will replace us, but because it can work alongside us, amplifying human creativity and productivity in ways we've yet to imagine.

AI in Your Pocket: Everyday Tools at Your Fingertips

Imagine having a magical toolkit that fits right in your pocket, always ready to spring into action. You don't need a wand or spellbook, just a few AI applications that work wonders with a few taps on your smartphone. Let's start with ChatGPT, a text generation marvel that transforms your vague thoughts into eloquent prose. Whether you're writing a heartfelt birthday message or crafting a last-minute email to your boss, ChatGPT is like having a silver-tongued friend whispering in your ear, ensuring every word hits the mark with style and grace. And it doesn't stop there; for those moments when creativity strikes after staring at a blank page for hours, ChatGPT is there to spark your imagination with ideas that flow as smoothly as your morning coffee.

Next up, Canva. The graphic design genius that turns the average Jane or Joe into a veritable Picasso. With its treasure trove of design suggestions, Canva's intuitive interface feels like a personal art studio, minus the mess of paint spills and paper cuts. Drag and drop elements with the ease of a seasoned artist, and let Canva's AI do the heavy lifting by suggesting layouts that are nothing short of spectacular. Whether you're whipping up an invitation, a social media post, or even a business presentation, Canva ensures you're always the star of the show, earning you accolades for your newfound design prowess. It's the kind of magic trick that leaves people wondering, "How did they do that?"

And then there's Dall-e, the digital artist who never sleeps. Need an image of a cat juggling oranges on Mars? Dall-e's got you covered. It's perfect for those moments when words alone can't capture your vision, and you need an image that speaks louder than a thousand tweets. Creating unique visuals for presentations, blogs, or that quirky birthday gift has never been easier or more entertaining. Dall-e is like having an art gallery at your fingertips, ready to showcase your wildest ideas in vibrant color.

These tools are designed with you in mind, ensuring a user-friendly experience that even the most tech-averse can navigate. Pre-set templates and suggestions remove the guesswork, allowing you to focus on what you do best—being creative and productive. No need to fear the technology; embrace it as you would a helpful neighbor who always knows just what you need. It's technology that works for you, not the other way around.

To really make the most of these tools, consider customizing settings to fit your unique style and needs. Like a tailored suit, a little adjustment here and there ensures the perfect fit. Dive into the settings and tweak them until they feel just right. And don't forget about the vibrant online communities buzzing with users just like you. Engage with these communities to share tips, seek advice, or simply marvel at what others are creating. It's like a virtual playground where everyone's invited, and you never know what new trick you'll learn next.

So, there you have it. A pocketful of AI tools ready to make your life easier, your work more efficient, and your creative projects more dazzling than ever. No need to be a tech whiz; just someone curious enough to give it a shot. You might just find yourself wondering how you ever managed without them.

AI for All Ages: Making Technology Accessible

Picture a world where technology isn't just for the tech-savvy youth but is embraced by everyone, from sprightly toddlers to wise seniors. Imagine your grandmother wearing a smartwatch that doesn't just tell time but also keeps an eye on her heart rate, or your child using a fun, interactive app to learn fractions while giggling at virtual characters. This vision of inclusivity in AI isn't just a dream—it's happening right now. AI is here to break down barriers and make life a little brighter for all age groups. For seniors, AI offers health monitoring tools that act like a vigilant guardian angel, keeping tabs on vitals and reminding them to take their medication. Products like wearable health monitors empower seniors to maintain independence, offering peace of mind to their loved ones. These devices may not make them invincible, but they sure do give them a fighting chance at staying healthier longer.

Students, on the other hand, have found a new ally in AI for educational support. It's like having a tutor who never sleeps and doesn't mind explaining calculus for the umpteenth time. AI-driven educational tools provide personalized learning experiences, adapting to each student's pace and style. Whether it's mastering algebra or learning to code, these tools make education feel less like a chore and more like an adventure. With AI, students don't just memorize facts; they engage with material in a way that sticks. Imagine a classroom where each child learns at their own speed, and teachers have the tools to tailor lessons to individual needs. That's the magic of AI in education.

Now, let's talk resources. It's not just about throwing technology at the problem and hoping for the best. We need age-appropriate tools that cater to different needs. For the littlest ones, educational apps turn learning into a game, making topics like math and science as exciting as a treasure hunt. Meanwhile, seniors can enjoy AI-driven games designed to keep their minds sharp and engaged. These aren't just your run-of-the-mill puzzles; they're crafted to challenge and stimulate, providing cognitive exercise that feels like playtime. Whether it's a crossword puzzle that updates in real time or a memory game that adjusts difficulty based on performance, these tools are both fun and beneficial.

But what truly sets AI apart is its ability to bring people together. Family projects using AI tools can transform an ordinary weekend into an extraordinary bonding experience. Imagine the joy of creating a digital family photo album with AI-generated captions or building a family tree with virtual reality. Community workshops on AI literacy can foster a sense of camaraderie, where neighbors gather to learn and explore together. These workshops aren't just about learning; they're about creating connections and sparking curiosity. They break down the myths and fears surrounding AI, replacing them with knowledge and empowerment.

Of course, no technology is without its hurdles. Common barriers to AI adoption include fear of the unknown and a lack of confidence in using new tools. But these can be overcome with simplified tutorials designed to be as approachable as a chat with a friend. Workshops aimed at demystifying technology fears can turn skeptics into enthusiasts. By addressing these concerns head-on, we can transform apprehension into enthusiasm, paving the way for a future where AI is as familiar as a cup of coffee.

In this vibrant tapestry of life, AI isn't just another thread; it's the needle that stitches us together, weaving connections across generations. So, whether you're a senior wanting to stay independent, a student eager to learn, or a parent looking to connect with your kids in new ways, AI has something to offer. It's not just about technology—it's about making life richer, brighter, and a whole lot more fun.

Chapter Two

Practical AI Applications for Daily Life

Ever feel like your calendar has a mind of its own, plotting to keep you in endless meetings, appointments, and tasks? Fear not, because AI has swooped in to rescue us from the chaos of our own schedules. Welcome to the age of smart scheduling, where AI doesn't just organize your time; it crafts it into a well-oiled machine. Imagine having a personal assistant who never sleeps, never takes a coffee break, and always knows when you're about to double-book yourself. It's like having a sixth sense for time management. Welcome to a world where AI helps you reclaim your day, one smart suggestion at a time.

AI-powered scheduling tools are the unsung heroes of productivity, silently optimizing your time like a backstage crew in a theater. With applications like Google Calendar and Clockwise, your schedule transforms from a chaotic mess into a symphony of efficiency. Google Calendar, for instance, doesn't just plot events; it recommends the best times based on your habits and preferences. It's like having a friend who's always one step ahead, gently nudging you toward a more organized life. Clockwise takes it a notch higher, optimizing internal meetings and carving out focus time so you can actually get work done without interruption. It's the virtual equivalent of putting a "Do Not Disturb" sign on your brain.

But why stop at just scheduling? AI can also automate reminders and prioritize tasks, ensuring you never miss another deadline or forget your cousin's birthday. With smart reminders, it's like having a tiny assistant perched on your shoulder, whispering gentle nudges about upcoming tasks. Meanwhile, AI-generated priority lists help you focus on what truly matters, pushing less urgent tasks to the back burner. Imagine waking up to find your day neatly planned out, with tasks prioritized based on urgency and importance. It's like having a personal life coach who knows exactly what you need to tackle first, without the nagging.

AI doesn't just manage your tasks; it tailors your entire day to fit your lifestyle. Personalization is where the magic happens, as AI-driven daily planners adjust themselves based on your past behavior. Do you work best in the morning? AI will slot your most demanding tasks then. Prefer a leisurely afternoon? Your planner will adapt, ensuring your schedule aligns with your natural rhythms. Customizable morning routines ensure you start each day on the right foot, whether that means yoga, coffee, or a quick scroll through the news.

Integrating AI with digital assistants like Alexa or Google Assistant brings a new level of seamless management. These trusty companions can update your calendar with a simple voice command, turning your words into action faster than you can say "schedule." Need to add a meeting while you're busy cooking dinner? Just speak up, and your assistant will handle it. It's hands-free scheduling at its finest, liberating your time for more important things, like perfecting your spaghetti sauce or helping with homework.

Try It Out: AI-Powered Scheduling Experiment

Why not give AI scheduling a whirl? Pick a tool like Google Calendar or Clockwise, and let it take the reins for a week. Set up your tasks, meetings, and appointments, and observe how the AI suggests organizing your time. Notice any patterns or improvements in your productivity? Reflect on how it feels to have a digital assistant making your life a bit easier. Keep track of any newfound free time and consider what you might do with it—read a book, take a walk, or finally tackle that hobby you've been putting off.

By embracing AI's scheduling prowess, you not only manage your time more effectively but also rediscover the joy of having time for yourself. It's like having a personal concierge who ensures you never miss a beat, leaving you with more time to enjoy the things that truly matter. So go ahead, let AI streamline your day, and watch as your once-overwhelming schedule transforms into a masterpiece of time management.

Home Automation: Simplifying Chores with AI

Imagine your home running like a well-oiled machine, where tedious tasks are magically taken care of without you lifting a finger. Welcome to the world of home automation, where AI is the invisible butler you never knew you needed. Picture this: a robotic vacuum cleaner, like the trusty Roomba, gliding effortlessly across your floors, picking up crumbs and dust bunnies with the precision of a ballet dancer. It's like having a cleaning service on retainer, minus the awkward small talk.

These clever devices map your home, learning every nook and cranny, ensuring not a speck of dirt escapes their path. And if gardening feels like wrestling with nature, smart gardening systems can take over, watering your plants and even suggesting when to plant those pesky tulips. It's gardening for those of us whose thumbs are more black than green.

But let's not stop at cleanliness. A fortress isn't complete without its defenses, and AI has revolutionized home security, making it both sophisticated and user-friendly. Imagine security cameras that don't just watch, but also recognize faces. Yes, those are AI-powered cameras with facial recognition, distinguishing between friends, foes, and the mail carrier. Meanwhile, smart locks with AI monitoring ensure that you never have to fumble for keys again. They offer peace of mind, knowing that your home is secure, even when you're miles away. These locks can be controlled remotely, so if you ever forget to lock up, a quick tap on your smartphone will do the trick. It's like having the ultimate bouncer at your door, without the need for a velvet rope.

And who doesn't love saving a bit of cash on those pesky energy bills? Smart devices like thermostats and lighting systems are here to help. Take Nest, for instance, a thermostat that learns your habits and adjusts the temperature accordingly. It's like having a personal climate concierge, ensuring your home is just the right temperature, whether you're there or not. Energy-efficient lighting systems, controlled by AI, dim or brighten based on the time of day and your activities. These systems don't just save power; they set the mood, turning your living room into a cozy nook or a vibrant party space with a simple voice command. It's intelligent living, minus the hefty utility bill.

All these AI gadgets don't work in isolation; they're part of a larger, harmonious ecosystem. Platforms like SmartThings provide central-ized control, allowing you to manage all your devices from a single app. It's like having a universal remote for your entire home. This synchronization means that when you say "Goodnight," your house knows to lock the doors, turn off the lights, and set the thermostat to your preferred sleeping temperature. Cross-device integration makes life simpler, connecting everything from your fridge to your security cameras. It's a symphony of technology, playing in perfect harmony to make your life easier and more enjoyable.

As you welcome AI into your home, you're not just upgrading your appliances; you're transforming your lifestyle. The convenience and efficiency are unmatched, allowing you to focus on what truly matters, whether that's spending time with family, pursuing hobbies, or simply relaxing. AI home automation isn't just about gadgets; it's about creating a living environment that supports and enhances your everyday life. So, go ahead and embrace the future, one smart device at a time.

Personal Finance: Managing Money with AI Tools

Imagine having a financial advisor who not only never sleeps but also costs less than your daily cup of coffee. Welcome to the age of AI-driven financial tools, where budgeting and saving become as effortless as snapping your fingers. Picture tools like Mint, which swoops in like a financial superhero, tracking your spending habits with the precision of a seasoned accountant. It categorizes every penny you spend, providing insights that make you wonder how you ever managed before. This isn't just about adding up numbers; it's about understanding your financial health in a way that's both enlightening and empowering.

Then there's Digit, an AI savings app that works its magic by analyzing your spending patterns and automatically setting aside money for you. It's like having a savvy piggy bank that knows when to save and when to let you splurge a little. With Digit, saving becomes a background task you barely notice, yet it accumulates wealth over time. You don't have to think about it, which is probably why it's so effective. You simply wake up one day with a tidy sum saved up, and suddenly that vacation or emergency fund doesn't seem so out of reach.

But AI isn't just about saving what you already have; it can also help you grow your wealth. Enter robo-advisors like Betterment, which offer investment advice without the hefty fees of traditional advisors. These tools analyze market trends and suggest investment strategies tailored to your financial goals. It's as if you have a Wall Street guru in your pocket, guiding you through the often intimidating world of stocks and bonds. AI stock analysis tools further aid your decision-making by providing real-time data and insights that help you make informed choices. Whether you're a seasoned investor or a curious newbie, these tools offer a level of financial literacy and empowerment that was once reserved for the financial elite.

Keeping track of where your money goes is just as important as knowing how to grow it. AI excels at monitoring expenses and spending habits, helping you stay on top of your finances with minimal effort. Expense categorization apps automatically sort your transactions into neat categories, offering a snapshot of your spending habits at a glance. It's like having a financial diary that writes itself, highlighting patterns you might not have noticed. Coupled with spending habit visualization tools, you can see exactly where your money tends to disappear, helping you make smarter choices about where to cut back or invest more.

Financial literacy is crucial in today's world, and AI is here to educate you without the need for evening classes or dry textbooks. AI chatbots offer financial advice with the patience of a saint, answering questions and offering tips as you navigate the complex world of personal finance. They're like having a mentor who's always available, ready to guide you through the intricacies of budgeting, saving, and investing. Personalized financial education platforms further enhance your understanding by offering tailored lessons that cater to your specific needs and knowledge level. Whether you're planning for retirement or just trying to stretch your paycheck a little further, these tools provide the knowledge and confidence you need to take control of your financial future.

In the realm of personal finance, AI acts as both a guide and a tool, helping you navigate the often daunting world of money management. It takes the guesswork out of budgeting, saving, and investing, offering insights and strategies that were once the domain of financial experts. By embracing these AI tools, you're not just managing your money; you're mastering it, with the ease and confidence of someone who knows exactly where their financial future is headed.

AI in the Kitchen: Recipes and Meal Planning

Imagine transforming your kitchen into a culinary command center where meal planning and cooking become as streamlined as a well-practiced dance. Gone are the days of staring into the fridge, hoping inspiration strikes before the milk expires. With AI on your side, you have tools like the Paprika app at your fingertips, ready to whisk you away into a world where meal planning is more science than guesswork. Paprika doesn't just help you organize recipes; it customizes meal plans that fit your dietary preferences and schedules them seamlessly into your routine. It's like having a personal chef who's always on call, without the hefty price tag or need for a spacious pantry.

AI-driven recipe generators take this convenience a step further by offering an array of culinary possibilities with the click of a button. These tools analyze your preferences, dietary restrictions, and even what's already in your pantry. Imagine typing in "chicken and broccoli," and voilà, a gourmet meal plan appears, complete with cooking instructions and a digital shopping list. It's like having a culinary wizard at your disposal, conjuring delicious options that cater to your every whim and nutritional need. Say goodbye to the monotony of repeated meals and hello to a diverse menu that's as easy to execute as it is to enjoy.

For those who fancy themselves the next Julia Child or Gordon Ramsay, AI is more than just a planner—it's a teacher. With AI cooking assistants like Chef Watson, you can explore new recipes and refine your cooking techniques with interactive tutorials that guide you step by step. These virtual sous-chefs offer suggestions, correct mistakes, and even propose flavor pairings you might not have considered. Imagine having a mentor who patiently walks you through the intricacies of soufflés or the delicate balance of spices in a curry. With AI, you can expand your culinary repertoire and impress dinner guests with dishes that are as sophisticated as they are satisfying.

Grocery shopping, once a necessary evil, is now an efficient endeavor thanks to smart grocery list apps. These AI-powered tools streamline your shopping trips by generating lists based on your meal plans and dietary needs. They even offer price comparisons, ensuring you get the best deals without the hassle of clipping coupons or visiting multiple stores. Picture yourself breezing through the aisles, list in hand, knowing that you've got everything you need for the week without breaking the bank. It's like having a savvy shopping assistant who knows when to splurge on organic kale and when to stick with the store brand.

Personalized dietary recommendations are another boon of AI technology, tailoring nutrition advice to your unique health profile. AI nutrition apps analyze data from health-tracking devices, providing insights that help you make informed choices about what to eat. Whether you're managing a health condition, training for a marathon, or just trying to fit into those jeans from last summer, AI offers guidance that's as precise as a tailor's measuring tape. These apps are like having a dietitian in your pocket, ready to offer advice on portion sizes, calorie intake, and even suggest healthy swaps to keep your meals both nutritious and delicious.

As you integrate AI into your kitchen, you're not just simplifying meal prep; you're enhancing your culinary experience. It's about creating a kitchen environment where innovation and tradition coexist, where the everyday becomes extraordinary, and where time spent cooking is as enjoyable as the meals themselves. Whether you're a seasoned cook or a kitchen novice, AI offers tools that transform cooking from a chore into a creative and fulfilling pursuit.

Health and Wellness: AI for a Better You

In today's fast-paced world, keeping fit and healthy can sometimes feel like trying to catch a runaway train. Luckily, AI technologies have stepped in to ensure you don't have to sprint just to keep up. Picture AI fitness apps like MyFitnessPal, your personal trainer that fits snugly in your pocket. It tracks your workouts, calories, and even suggests ways to improve your fitness routine. It's like having a fitness coach who's always there, offering encouragement and advice without ever needing a water break. Pair that with wearable fitness trackers, and you've got a dynamic duo that not only counts your steps but also monitors your heart rate, sleep patterns, and more, providing insights that help you make smarter health choices. These gadgets aren't just accessories; they're your partners in achieving those fitness goals you've been chasing.

Mental well-being is just as crucial as physical health, and AI is proving to be a valuable ally in this arena as well. Think of AI mental health apps like Woebot as your friendly neighborhood therapist, ready to chat whenever you need to vent or seek guidance. Unlike traditional therapy, Woebot is available 24/7, offering strategies to manage stress, anxiety, and other mental health challenges with a gentle, conversational approach. Meanwhile, meditation apps with AI-guided sessions help users find their inner calm, reducing stress with personalized meditative practices. These apps are like having a Zen master on speed dial, guiding you through mindfulness exercises that center your thoughts and soothe your soul. In a world that often feels chaotic, these AI tools are the calm amidst the storm.

Keeping an eye on your health metrics has never been easier, thanks to AI devices that monitor and analyze vital health data. Imagine a smartwatch that does more than just tell time; it's a health hub that tracks your heart rate, activity levels, and sleep quality. It's like wearing a tiny doctor on your wrist, offering real-time health insights that you can act on immediately. AI-powered blood pressure monitors take it a step further, allowing you to keep track of your blood pressure from the comfort of your home. These devices offer the convenience of regular monitoring without the hassle of doctor's appointments, empowering you to take proactive steps in managing your health.

AI doesn't just offer raw data; it provides personalized health insights that help you make informed decisions about your well-being. AI-driven health assessment platforms analyze your data to offer tailored advice and recommendations. Whether it's suggesting a new workout plan or offering dietary tips, these platforms are like having a personal health consultant who knows your body as well as you do. Personalized fitness coaching with AI guidance ensures that your fitness journey is customized to your unique needs and goals. It's like having a bespoke fitness plan, crafted just for you, that adapts as you progress, ensuring you always have the right support to reach your objectives.

As we embrace AI in our health and wellness routines, we find that it's not just about the technology; it's about enhancing our quality of life. These tools provide the insights and guidance we need to live healthier, more fulfilling lives. They empower us to make informed decisions, prioritize our well-being, and achieve balance in an often hectic world. With AI by your side, you're not just monitoring your health; you're actively improving it, one smart choice at a time.

In this chapter, we've explored the transformative power of AI in daily life, from time management to personal wellness. As we look forward, consider how these practical applications of AI not only simplify tasks but enrich our lives in unexpected ways. The next chapter will delve into how AI is revolutionizing creativity and the arts, opening new avenues for expression and innovation. Keep turning those pages, as we continue to uncover the fascinating ways AI can enhance our human experience.

Chapter Three

AI in Creativity and the Arts

D id you ever dream of being an artist but feel more like a doodler than a Da Vinci? Fear not! In the magical world of AI, creativity is no longer a talent reserved for the select few who can tell the difference between a Picasso and a Pollock. Thanks to platforms like Canva and Dall-e, art is as accessible as a carton of milk in the fridge—and almost as easy to spill. These digital powerhouses are not just for the tech-savvy; they're designed for everyone who has ever had a creative itch they couldn't quite scratch. Whether you want to design a birthday card or create a masterpiece worthy of the Louvre, these tools are here to transform even your most modest artistic dreams into reality.

Canva is the Swiss Army knife of graphic design, offering a smorgasbord of options that can turn anyone into a visual virtuoso. Its AI-driven design suggestions act like a digital muse, gently nudging your creativity in the right direction. Imagine having a friendly assistant who never judges your font choices and always recommends the perfect color palette to make your project pop. From Magic Write to Magic Eraser, Canva's suite of AI tools is like having a team of little design elves working tirelessly behind the scenes to enhance your creations. Need to swap a background? No problem. Want to magically animate your presentation? Canva has got your back. With these tools, you can craft everything from social media posts to wedding invitations with the finesse of a seasoned designer.

Then there's Dall-e, an AI image generator that brings a touch of whimsy to the creative process. Picture typing a simple text prompt like "a panda playing a guitar on the moon" and watching as Dall-e conjures an image straight out of a surreal dream. It's like having a genie in your computer, ready to grant your visual wishes with a flick of its digital wand. Dall-e's power lies in its ability to generate stunning visuals from even the most outlandish ideas, making it perfect for those moments when your imagination runs wild. Whether you're designing a book cover or creating a quirky illustration for your blog, Dall-e's capabilities are as boundless as your creativity.

The beauty of AI tools like Canva and Dall-e is that they democratize art creation, making it accessible to anyone with a spark of inspiration. You don't need a degree in fine arts or years of practice to create something beautiful. These platforms feature user-friendly interfaces that guide you through the process, offering pre-made templates and AI-generated elements that simplify design tasks. It's like having a coloring book where you can color outside the lines and still end up with a masterpiece. With AI by your side, you can explore new styles and techniques without the fear of failure. Want to try your hand at abstract art? Go ahead. AI's got your back with style transfer techniques that let you experiment with a variety of artistic styles.

AI doesn't just enhance creativity; it acts as an invaluable collaborator in the artistic process. Imagine having access to AI-generated mood boards that inspire your next project or color palette suggestions tailored to your artistic preferences. These tools open up a world of possibilities, encouraging experimentation and innovation. Artists can push the boundaries of traditional art, creating pieces that are as unique as they are captivating. AI offers the freedom to explore without limits, allowing you to try new things and discover your artistic voice. Whether you're a seasoned artist looking to break new ground or a novice eager to learn, AI provides the tools and support to unleash your creativity like never before.

Explore Your Creativity: Try It Yourself!

Wondering how these tools can spark your creativity? Take a moment to explore Canva's Magic Design or Dall-e's image generation. Start with a simple project, like designing a birthday card or creating a unique digital illustration. Let the AI suggest elements, colors, and layouts, and watch as your ideas come to life. As you experiment, notice how AI enhances your creativity, offering new perspectives and possibilities. Keep your creations in a digital portfolio to track your progress and see how your artistic skills evolve over time.

The Music of AI: Composing with MidJourney

Imagine a world where composing music doesn't require years of practice or the ability to read sheet music. Enter MidJourney, an AI tool that revolutionizes how we think about music composition. With MidJourney, you can create melodies and harmonies without having to differentiate between a treble clef and a bass clef. It's like having a digital muse that never gets tired or runs out of ideas. MidJourney generates music based on mood, adapting its compositions to fit whatever vibe you're aiming for—be it a relaxing afternoon tea or a high-energy workout session. The AI analyzes existing patterns in music to produce something entirely new, providing melodies that feel both fresh and familiar.

The process of creating music with AI might sound daunting, but MidJourney simplifies it with user-friendly interfaces. You don't need to be a tech wizard to start composing. Just imagine having a musical canvas before you, and MidJourney as the brush that paints notes across it. Integration with digital audio workstations (DAWs) means you can easily refine your AI-generated tunes, adding personal touches or collaborating with others. The interface is intuitive, guiding you through the process like a patient teacher who never rolls their eyes when you hit the wrong note. It's music composition made accessible to everyone, where even the tech-averse can feel like a maestro.

AI doesn't just stop at generating tunes; it acts as a creative partner, inspiring new musical ideas and collaborations. Think of it as a jam session where the AI brings infinite potential to the table. It suggests chord progressions, riffs, and even entire compositions that can spark your creativity. Musicians can use AI for collaborative projects, allowing them to explore areas they might never have ventured into alone. This partnership can lead to generative music projects, where AI continuously evolves the sound, keeping it dynamic and engaging. It's like having a bandmate who never misses a beat and always has a new riff to try.

One of the most exciting aspects of using AI in music is its ability to expand musical possibilities, helping musicians explore new genres and styles. Imagine dabbling in jazz, then effortlessly transitioning to electronic dance music, with AI guiding you through the nuances of each genre. MidJourney encourages cross-genre experiments, blending elements from different musical traditions to create something entirely unique. AI-generated soundscapes push the boundaries of conventional music, creating immersive auditory experiences that captivate and inspire. It's like having a musical passport that lets you explore the rich tapestry of global sounds without ever leaving your living room.

Incorporating AI into music composition is not about replacing musicians but augmenting their capabilities. It's a tool that complements traditional skills and encourages experimentation. Whether you're a seasoned composer looking to break new ground or a curious beginner eager to experiment, MidJourney offers the resources to explore music in innovative ways. AI unlocks a realm of creative potential, allowing anyone to express themselves through music, regardless of their technical skills or background. So, pick up your virtual baton, and let MidJourney take you on a musical adventure where the possibilities are as endless as the melodies it can create.

3.3 Writing with a Partner: ChatGPT as a Co-Author

Imagine sitting down to write and having an endless reservoir of ideas at your fingertips. Enter ChatGPT, your new writing partner, who never tires, never judges your grammar, and always has a fresh take on even the most mundane topics. Whether you're crafting the next great novel or simply trying to spice up this year's holiday letter, ChatGPT is here to help you conquer that dreaded blank page. Writer's block? Consider it a thing of the past. With ChatGPT, you can generate prompts that ignite your imagination and get those creative juices flowing. Need to brainstorm a story plot? ChatGPT is like having a brainstorming buddy who's always ready to throw around ideas, no matter how wild or unconventional.

ChatGPT's role doesn't stop at inspiration. It can also act as a co-author when crafting narratives. Picture this: you're writing a dialogue between two characters, but their conversation feels stilted, lacking the natural ebb and flow of real speech. Enter ChatGPT, ready to suggest dialogue that brings your characters to life with wit and authenticity. Perhaps you're developing a character's backstory and need a fresh perspective; ChatGPT offers insights that add depth and dimension, ensuring your characters aren't just two-dimensional figures but living, breathing individuals with rich histories and motivations. It's like having an extra brain at your disposal, one that's always teeming with possibilities.

Once your story starts to take shape, ChatGPT proves invaluable in the editing and proofreading stages. Is your grammar a little rusty? ChatGPT's got you covered, offering grammar and style suggestions that polish your prose until it shines. Those complex sentences that seem to twist and turn without end? ChatGPT can rephrase them, making your writing clearer and more concise. It's like having a personal editor who never misses a comma or a misplaced modifier. Even the pros need a second pair of eyes, and ChatGPT is like having an eagle-eyed friend who's more than willing to help refine your work.

But what if you're writing for a specific audience or adapting your content across different genres? ChatGPT can tailor your writing projects to fit specific themes or tones. Want to write a mystery with just the right amount of suspense? ChatGPT can help you nail that tone. Need to adapt a story for a younger audience? It can suggest language and style adjustments so your content resonates with readers of all ages. It's like having a chameleon that can change hues to fit any narrative landscape, ensuring your voice remains authentic while adapting to various contexts.

In essence, ChatGPT is not just a tool but an extension of your creative self, enhancing your writing process every step of the way. It offers a unique blend of creativity and functionality, making it a perfect companion for writers of all levels. Whether you're penning poetry, crafting a screenplay, or simply trying to express a deeply personal story, ChatGPT is there to support, inspire, and elevate your writing to new heights. With it by your side, you have the freedom to explore, create, and refine your work with confidence and flair.

Ideogram for Visual Storytelling

Imagine a world where you can tell stories not just with words, but with vibrant, compelling visuals that leap off the page. This is where Ideogram steps in, transforming your storytelling into a visual feast. Think of it as a digital paintbrush that lets you craft narratives with images rather than paragraphs. Ideogram helps you create AI-generated storyboards that capture the essence of your narrative with minimal input. You type in a few key details, and voila, the AI conjures up a storyboard that looks like it was plucked straight from a director's sketchbook. It's like having a creative genie at your disposal, ready to illustrate your ideas as fast as you can dream them up.

Visual storytelling is all about elevating the narrative with imagery, and with AI, this becomes a breeze. Whether you're illustrating key plot points or designing characters and settings, AI simplifies the process. Picture this: you're developing a fantasy story and need to bring a mystical forest to life. With AI, you can create a lush, enchanted woodland teeming with life, without ever picking up a paintbrush. It's as if you have an entire animation studio working tirelessly to bring your vision to fruition. The visuals can be detailed and dynamic, providing depth and dimension to your story in a way that words alone sometimes can't.

The beauty of using AI in visual storytelling is the freedom it offers to experiment with different styles. Fancy trying your hand at a noir-style detective story? Or maybe a vibrant, Pixar-like animation? AI's diverse art style generation lets you play with visual themes and adapt your storytelling to fit any genre or mood. This flexibility encourages creativity, allowing you to try new things without the fear of making permanent mistakes. It's like having a wardrobe full of costumes, each one transforming your story into something fresh and exciting. You can easily switch from a gritty, monochrome look to a colorful, whimsical design, all with a few clicks.

For those of you without a formal art background, AI tools like Ideogram are a boon for non-traditional storytellers. You don't need to be an expert with a paintbrush or a graphics tablet. Simplified visual creation processes mean that anyone, regardless of skill level, can become a storyteller. It's like having a set of training wheels that help you find your balance before you take off on your own creative journey. AI assistance can even help amateur filmmakers, enabling them to storyboard and create visual narratives with ease. You can focus on the story you want to tell, while the AI handles the technical details of bringing it to life visually.

Ideogram's capability to support storytelling doesn't just lie in creating pretty pictures. It's about creating a cohesive visual narrative that complements your story. The AI works like a seasoned cinematographer, suggesting angles, lighting, and compositions that enhance the emotional impact of your tale. Whether you're crafting a children's book, a graphic novel, or a short film, AI can help you ensure that your visuals align seamlessly with your narrative goals. It's not just about telling a story; it's about creating an immersive experience that engages your audience on multiple levels. As you wield this tool, you'll find that visual storytelling is not only more accessible but also more powerful than ever before.

Designing Your Space: AI in Interior Design

Imagine stepping into your home and feeling like you've entered a space that perfectly reflects your personality, comfort preferences, and style ambitions. Thanks to AI, this isn't just a dream reserved for those with a knack for design or a hefty budget for decorators. AI applications have taken the guesswork out of interior design, transforming the daunting task of redecorating into an enjoyable and accessible experience. Tools like virtual room planners allow you to rearrange furniture, test different layouts, and even knock down virtual walls—all without lifting a finger or breaking a sweat. It's like having an interior designer in your pocket, always ready with suggestions and ideas to make your space shine.

Imagine AI-generated decor suggestions popping up on your screen, tailored specifically to your tastes. Whether you're a fan of mid-century modern or prefer the cozy charm of cottagecore, AI has you covered. These recommendations consider everything from the color of your walls to the amount of natural light that filters through your windows. They offer insights as if they know you better than your closest friends, suggesting pieces that fit seamlessly into your existing décor. It's like having a personal shopper who understands your style better than you do, with the added bonus of never rolling their eyes at your choices.

Personalization is where AI truly shines, making home design as unique as the individuals who inhabit each space. Customizable design templates allow you to tweak every element until it feels just right, ensuring your home doesn't look like a page torn from a catalog. But the magic doesn't end there. AI-driven color and material matching takes personalization to the next level. By analyzing your preferences, these tools suggest color schemes and materials that harmonize with your vision, turning your ideas into reality. It's like having a color wheel and fabric swatch at your fingertips, ready to create a space that's both cohesive and personalized.

Visualization is a game-changer in the world of interior design. AI enhances this process with 3D rendering of room designs, allowing you to see your ideas come to life before committing to any changes. You can virtually walk through your redesigned space, experiencing the flow and functionality from the comfort of your couch. This virtual reality walkthrough is like a test drive for your home, letting you ensure every detail is perfect before making it permanent. It saves you from the dreaded "Why did I choose that wallpaper?" moments and gives you the confidence to make bold design choices.

Sustainability is more than just a buzzword; it's a necessity in today's world. AI plays a crucial role in promoting eco-friendly and sustainable interior design. With recommendations for sustainable materials and energy-efficient design solutions, AI helps you create a space that's not only beautiful but also kind to the planet. Whether it's selecting bamboo flooring or choosing energy-saving lighting options, AI empowers you to make choices that align with your values. It's like having an environmental consultant guiding your every move, ensuring that your home is as green as it is gorgeous.

As we wrap up our exploration of AI in creativity and the arts, consider how these tools empower us to express ourselves in new ways, whether it's through music, writing, storytelling, or design. AI opens doors to possibilities once limited to those with specific skills or resources, democratizing creativity and making it accessible to all. In the next chapter, we'll delve into how AI is transforming productivity in the workplace, offering tools and techniques that streamline processes and enhance efficiency. Stay tuned as we continue to uncover the ways AI is reshaping our world, one innovative step at a time.

Chapter Four

Mastering ChatGPT

A Step-by-Step Guide to Writing Effective Communications with Specialized Prompts

Effective communication is the foundation of success in both personal and professional life. Whether crafting an email, writing a blog post, preparing an employment contract, or drafting a white paper, clarity and precision are essential. ChatGPT can be a powerful tool for generating well-structured, engaging, and professional content with the right prompts.

This tutorial will guide you through:

- How to use ChatGPT effectively for communication

- Structuring prompts for clarity and effectiveness

- Advanced techniques for refining AI-generated responses

- Ten sample prompts for different types of communication

By the end of this guide, you will be able to create compelling written content tailored to various audiences and objectives.

Understanding ChatGPT for Effective Writing

ChatGPT is a conversational AI designed to generate human-like text based on prompts. It can be used for business communication, creative writing, academic research, legal documentation, and much more.

Key Features of ChatGPT for Communication

1. **Adaptability** – Can write in various tones, from formal to conversational.

2. **Customization** – Can generate content based on specific guidelines and requirements.

3. **Speed** – Produces drafts quickly, saving time in content creation.

4. **Consistency** – Ensures a uniform tone and style across different types of documents.

5. **Refinement** – Can edit and improve content based on feedback.

To harness ChatGPT's full potential, it is crucial to craft well-structured prompts.

How to Write Effective Prompts

A well-structured prompt helps ChatGPT understand the context and deliver better results.

Elements of a Strong Prompt

1. **Specify the Type of Communication** – Clearly state whether you need an email, report, letter, or contract.

2. **Define the Purpose** – Mention the goal of the communication (e.g., informing, persuading, apologizing).

3. **Indicate the Audience** – Provide details on the intended reader (e.g., a manager, customer, partner).

4. **Set the Tone and Style** – Indicate whether the text should be formal, casual, persuasive, or friendly.

5. **Provide Key Details** – Include relevant information such as names, dates, and specific points to cover.

Advanced Techniques for Refining ChatGPT's Responses

1. **Use Iterative Refinement** – If the first response is not perfect, provide feedback and ask for improvements. Example: "Make this email more concise and persuasive."

2. **Ask for Multiple Versions** – Request different styles or tones and choose the best one. Example: "Rewrite this as a more professional and concise version."

3. **Incorporate Data and Examples** – Provide specific figures or case studies to add depth to the generated content.

4. **Use Formatting Instructions** – Request bullet points, numbered lists, or sections for better readability.

Ten Sample Prompts for Different Communications

Below are ten specialized prompts you can use to generate well-crafted written content in various formats.

1. Professional Email (Formal Business Communication)

Prompt:
"Write a professional email to a client informing them about a delay in project delivery due to unforeseen circumstances. Maintain a polite and apologetic tone, provide a revised timeline, and assure them of our commitment to quality."

2. Blog Post (Engaging and Informative)

Prompt:
"Write a 1,000-word blog post on 'The Future of Remote Work and

How Companies Can Adapt.' Include an introduction, key trends, benefits and challenges, and a conclusion with actionable insights."

3. Employment Contract (Legal and Structured)

Prompt:

"Draft a standard employment contract for a new software developer hire. Include sections on job responsibilities, salary, benefits, working hours, confidentiality, termination policies, and a dispute resolution clause."

4. Romantic Letter (Personal and Affectionate)

Prompt:

"Write a heartfelt love letter to a partner expressing deep gratitude and appreciation for their support and kindness. Keep the tone warm, poetic, and intimate."

5. Thesis Outline (Academic and Detailed)

Prompt:

"Create a detailed thesis outline for a dissertation titled 'The Impact of Artificial Intelligence on Modern Healthcare.' Include an introduction, literature review, research methodology, expected findings, and conclusion."

6. White Paper (Technical and Authoritative)

Prompt:
"Write a white paper on 'The Role of Blockchain in Cybersecurity.' Include an executive summary, problem statement, solution overview, technical details, case studies, and a conclusion with future implications."

7. Apology Letter (Professional and Sincere)

Prompt:
"Write a formal apology letter from a company to a customer who experienced a defective product. Express regret, acknowledge the inconvenience caused, offer a replacement or refund, and reaffirm the company's commitment to quality and customer satisfaction."

8. Marketing Copy (Persuasive and Engaging)

Prompt:
"Create a compelling product description for a new smartwatch with health-tracking features, long battery life, and a sleek design. Highlight its unique selling points, target audience, and call-to-action."

9. Speech Script (Inspiring and Well-Structured)

Prompt:
"Write a 5-minute speech for a company CEO on 'Embracing In-

novation in a Fast-Changing Business Landscape.' Make it inspiring, forward-thinking, and motivational."

10. Business Proposal (Persuasive and Clear)

Prompt:
"Draft a business proposal for a startup seeking funding for a new AI-powered customer service chatbot. Include sections on company background, problem statement, solution, market potential, revenue model, competitive advantage, and funding requirements."

Best Practices for Using ChatGPT in Communication

1. **Start with a Clear Objective** – Be specific about what you need to ensure ChatGPT generates a useful response.

2. **Use Contextual Details** – Providing background information helps create a more relevant and personalized output.

3. **Request Multiple Versions** – Ask ChatGPT to generate different styles so you can choose the best one.

4. **Edit and Personalize** – AI-generated text should be refined to align with your voice and style.

5. **Ensure Legal and Ethical Accuracy** – Always review AI-generated contracts, policies, or official documents to ensure compliance with legal standards.

Final Thoughts

ChatGPT is a powerful tool for crafting effective communication across various formats. Whether you need a professional email, a persuasive business proposal, or a heartfelt love letter, structured prompts can help generate high-quality text quickly and efficiently.

By understanding how to frame prompts, refining AI responses, and customizing content for specific audiences, you can enhance the clarity, impact, and professionalism of your written communications.

Experiment with different prompts, refine the responses, and use ChatGPT as a reliable writing assistant to elevate your communication skills.

Chapter Five

AI-Driven Design: Elevating Creativity with Ideogram

A Step-by-Step Guide to Creating Stunning AI Images

Artificial Intelligence has transformed the way people create images, and Ideogram is one of the most powerful AI tools for generating high-quality visuals. Whether you are an artist, designer, marketer, or someone who simply enjoys creating, Ideogram provides an intuitive way to produce unique and engaging images through well-crafted text prompts.

This guide will walk you through what Ideogram is, how to use it effectively, techniques to refine your prompts for better results, and ten detailed example prompts to help you generate stunning AI images.

What is Ideogram?

Ideogram is an advanced AI-powered image generation tool that allows users to create high-quality visuals by providing simple or complex text descriptions. Unlike many other AI image generators, Ideogram excels at integrating text into images while maintaining artistic quality. It also offers various styles, from photorealistic to anime, cyberpunk, watercolor, and more.

Some of Ideogram's key features include its ability to incorporate readable text into images, generate highly detailed photorealistic compositions, provide multiple artistic styles, and allow creative control over aspect ratios and image complexity.

How to Use Ideogram Effectively

Step 1: Sign Up and Access the Platform

Visit ideogram.ai and create an account. Once you log in, you can access the image generation dashboard, where you can enter prompts to start creating images.

Step 2: Writing an Effective Prompt

A well-structured prompt ensures that Ideogram generates high-quality images. The best prompts contain specific details to help the AI understand your vision clearly.

An effective prompt includes the subject, style, lighting, color scheme, background, and additional elements. For example, instead of saying "a house," a more detailed prompt would be "a cozy wooden cabin in the snowy mountains, warm golden lights, ultra-detailed, hyperrealistic."

Step 3: Selecting the Right Image Size

Ideogram supports different aspect ratios, allowing users to create images tailored for specific purposes.

A 1024x1024 image is ideal for social media posts and profile pictures. A 1792x1024 image is best for landscapes, banners, or wallpapers. A 1024x1792 image works well for vertical compositions like mobile wallpapers or portraits.

To adjust the image size, specify the aspect ratio in your prompt or set it in the image generation settings before running the request.

Step 4: Generating and Refining the Image

After entering the prompt, selecting the image size, and choosing an artistic style, click the "Generate" button. The AI will process the request and display the results in a few seconds. If the image does not fully meet your expectations, you can refine your prompt by adding more specific details or requesting variations with slight adjustments.

Advanced Techniques for Creating Stunning AI Images

There are several techniques you can use to improve the quality and accuracy of AI-generated images in Ideogram.

Using descriptive adjectives enhances image quality. Instead of writing "a car," a better prompt would be "a futuristic sports car with glowing neon lights, ultra-detailed, cyberpunk aesthetic."

Experimenting with different styles can help achieve the desired look. Styles such as "3D render," "watercolor painting," "anime art," or "steampunk aesthetic" all produce distinct results.

Lighting can dramatically impact the mood of an image. Options like "dramatic lighting, golden hour, cinematic shadows, or moody ambiance" create different visual effects.

Camera angles and depth bring images to life. Including terms like "bird's-eye view, macro shot, wide-angle lens, depth of field, or bokeh effect" adds depth and perspective.

Specifying an art medium leads to unique styles. Options such as "hand-drawn sketch, digital painting, isometric pixel art, or cyberpunk aesthetic" allow for creative diversity.

Style Buttons

In Ideogram's prompt window, several style buttons allow you to tailor the generated images to specific artistic preferences:

1. **Auto**: This setting automatically selects the most appropriate style based on your prompt, streamlining the image generation process without manual style selection.

2. **General**: Ideal for a wide range of artistic creations, this style

excels in producing abstract paintings, pencil sketches, and computer-manipulated images, offering versatility for various creative projects.

3. **Realistic**: This style focuses on generating lifelike photographic images, capturing intricate details and textures to produce visuals that closely resemble real-world scenes.

4. **Design**: Tailored for graphic design needs, this style is perfect for creating logos, print-on-demand images, advertising flyers, menus, and other design-related visuals, ensuring clean and professional outputs.

5. **3D**: This style renders images with a three-dimensional appearance, making it suitable for generating characters, objects, and scenes that require depth and a realistic 3D effect.

6. **Anime**: Designed for enthusiasts of Japanese animation, this style generates images and characters reminiscent of popular anime, capturing the unique aesthetics and vibrant colors characteristic of the genre.

7. **Aspect Ratio**: This option allows you to define the proportional relationship between the width and height of your generated image. By selecting specific aspect ratios—such as 1:1 for squares, 16:9 for widescreen, or 9:16 for vertical formats—you can tailor images to fit various platforms and purposes, ensuring they meet your project's dimensional requirements.

8. **Magic Prompt**: This feature assists in crafting more detailed and imaginative prompts. When activated, Magic Prompt

analyzes your initial input and automatically expands it by adding descriptive elements, context, and stylistic nuances. This enhancement leads to richer and more accurate image outputs, especially beneficial when you're seeking inspiration or aiming to refine a basic idea into a comprehensive visual concept.

These style and dialog options provide users with the flexibility to produce images that align with their specific artistic vision and project requirements. Utilizing these tools effectively can significantly improve the quality and relevance of the images generated, aligning them closely with your creative vision.

Ten Example Prompts for Stunning AI Images

Below are ten detailed example prompts designed to help users create a variety of high-quality AI-generated images using Ideogram.

1. Cyberpunk City at Night (Wide: 1792x1024)

Prompt:
"A sprawling cyberpunk city illuminated by neon lights, flying cars zooming through the sky, massive digital billboards displaying futuristic advertisements, rain-soaked streets reflecting vibrant colors, dark sci-fi atmosphere, ultra-detailed, 8K cinematic lighting --ar 16:9"

2. Alien Jungle with Bioluminescent Plants (Square: 1024x1024)

Prompt:

"An exotic alien jungle at twilight, glowing bioluminescent plants casting an eerie blue light, towering twisted trees, mysterious floating creatures in the mist, deep and immersive science fiction environment, 8K ultra-detailed photorealism --ar 1:1"

3. Cosmic Wizard Summoning a Portal (Portrait: 1024x1792)

Prompt:

"A cosmic wizard standing atop a floating island in deep space, summoning an interdimensional portal with swirling galaxies inside, celestial energy crackling around him, majestic long robes, glowing staff, ultra-detailed magical realism, 8K fantasy art --ar 9:16"

4. Dragon vs. Spaceship Battle Over a Dying Star (Wide: 1792x1024)

Prompt:

"A high-intensity battle between a massive fire-breathing dragon and an advanced spaceship, set against the backdrop of a dying star exploding in supernova, energy blasts and flames colliding, epic science fantasy fusion, 8K ultra-detailed, cinematic lighting --ar 16:9"

5. Steampunk Airship Over a Floating City (Square: 1024x1024)

Prompt:

"A colossal steampunk airship hovering over a floating city in the clouds,

intricate brass gears and glowing blue energy engines, Victorian-style architecture suspended on floating rock islands, golden sunset lighting, ultra-detailed, 8K fantasy steampunk world --ar 1:1"

6. Galactic Warlord Overlooking His Empire (Wide: 1792x1024)

Prompt:

"A powerful galactic warlord in futuristic black armor, standing on a command deck overlooking a fleet of battleships, massive holographic star map floating in front of him, deep space battles unfolding in the distance, 8K cinematic science fiction, ultra-detailed --ar 16:9"

7. Ancient Ruins of a Lost Alien Civilization (Portrait: 1024x1792)

Prompt:

"Massive ancient ruins of a lost alien civilization, monolithic stone structures covered in glowing alien symbols, towering obelisks emitting soft ethereal light, abandoned futuristic technology overgrown with alien flora, misty atmosphere, 8K ultra-detailed, cinematic lighting --ar 9:16"

8. Battle Between a Cybernetic Knight and a Lava Titan (Wide: 1792x1024)

Prompt:

"An epic battle between a cybernetic knight in futuristic armor wielding an energy sword and a colossal molten lava titan, intense battlefield with

rivers of lava, crumbling ancient ruins, fiery explosions lighting up the sky, ultra-detailed 8K fantasy-science fiction hybrid --ar 16:9"

9. A Mystical Sorceress Channeling Cosmic Energy (Square: 1024x1024)

Prompt:

"A mystical sorceress with flowing silver hair, standing in a dark nebula, summoning cosmic energy in her hands, swirling galaxies and celestial magic forming around her, golden glowing eyes, radiant magical aura, hyper-detailed 8K fantasy art --ar 1:1"

10. An Explorer in an Ice Cave on an Alien Planet (Portrait: 1024x1792)

Prompt:

"A lone explorer in an advanced exosuit walking through a massive ice cave on an alien planet, glowing blue crystals embedded in the walls, a mysterious ancient artifact pulsing with energy, frozen alien structures in the distance, ultra-detailed 8K cinematic sci-fi adventure --ar 9:16"

Ten Example Prompts for Sales & Marketing

1. Minimalist Tech Company Logo (Square: 1024x1024)

Prompt:

"A sleek, modern technology company logo with a futuristic blue and

*silver color scheme, clean lines, abstract circuit design, professional and
minimalist branding, high-resolution 8K vector-style artwork, designed
for digital and print use --ar 1:1"*

2. Corporate Office Meeting with Two Professionals (Wide: 1792x1024)

Prompt:
*"A professional office meeting scene with two business professionals dis-
cussing strategy over a laptop, modern glass-wall office with city skyline
view, warm natural lighting, business casual attire, ultra-realistic 8K
corporate setting --ar 16:9"*

3. CEO Headshot with Dramatic Lighting (Portrait: 1024x1792)

Prompt:
*"A professional CEO headshot of a confident middle-aged executive in a
tailored navy blue suit, soft-focus corporate background, subtle cinematic
lighting on the face, high-resolution 8K photography, ultra-detailed and
realistic --ar 9:16"*

4. Creative Agency Brainstorming Session (Wide: 1792x1024)

Prompt:
*"A dynamic creative agency meeting with three diverse professionals
brainstorming ideas on a glass whiteboard, vibrant and modern work-*

space, coffee cups and laptops on the table, warm and energetic atmos-
phere, ultra-detailed 8K business setting --ar 16:9"

5. Elegant Fashion Brand Logo (Square: 1024x1024)

Prompt:
"A sophisticated and stylish fashion brand logo with a golden cursive
monogram, elegant minimalist design, luxury aesthetics, high-end ty-
pography, ultra-detailed 8K vector art, perfect for branding and print
--ar 1:1"

6. Office Desk Setup with Laptop and Coffee (Wide: 1792x1024)

Prompt:
"A minimalist and modern office desk setup with an open laptop, a
steaming coffee cup, a sleek smartphone, and a notepad, warm natural
morning light coming through the window, soft-focus background, ul-
tra-detailed 8K productivity workspace --ar 16:9"

7. Professional LinkedIn Headshot for Business Profile (Portrait: 1024x1792)

Prompt:
"A highly professional and polished LinkedIn profile headshot of a
young entrepreneur, smiling confidently, wearing a smart business suit,
blurred modern office background, soft and even lighting, ultra-detailed
8K photography, realistic and engaging --ar 9:16"

8. Startup Team Collaboration in a Modern Workspace (Wide: 1792x1024)

Prompt:

"A vibrant startup team collaboration scene in a modern coworking space, two men and one woman brainstorming on a project, laptop and notes on the table, casual but professional attire, engaging teamwork dynamic, ultra-detailed 8K corporate realism --ar 16:9"

9. Law Firm Logo with Elegant Gold and Black Design (Square: 1024x1024)

Prompt:

"A prestigious law firm logo with a golden scale of justice symbol, elegant serif typography, black and gold color scheme, strong and authoritative branding, ultra-detailed 8K vector design, professional and refined --ar 1:1"

10. Portrait of a Tech Professional in a Smart Office Environment (Portrait: 1024x1792)

Prompt:

"A professional headshot of a young tech engineer standing in a modern smart office, confident expression, casual tech industry attire, futuristic workspace with holographic displays in the background, ultra-detailed 8K cinematic photography --ar 9:16"

Thirty Advanced Commands You Can Use with Ideogram Prompts

Here are 10 useful Ideogram commands that work similarly to --ar (aspect ratio) and --dof (depth of field), allowing you to fine-tune and enhance AI-generated images.

1. **--q (Quality)** – Controls the rendering quality of the image. Higher values like --q 2 generate more detailed images but take longer to process.

2. **--v (Version)** – Specifies which version of the AI model to use. Example: --v 5.2 ensures the latest and most refined model is used.

3. **--stylize (Artistic Style Intensity)** – Adjusts how much artistic flair is added to the image. Example: --stylize 1000 adds more creative interpretation.

4. **--chaos (Creativity and Variation)** – Controls randomness in generation. Higher values like --chaos 50 produce more unexpected and unique outputs.

5. **--sref (Style Reference)** – Applies a specific style reference from an existing image or dataset. Example: --sref 12345 mimics a particular visual style.

6. **--tile (Seamless Pattern Mode)** – Generates seamless, repeating patterns useful for textures and backgrounds.

7. **--no (Negative Prompting)** – Excludes unwanted elements from the image. Example: --no text removes text from the final output.

8. **--w and --h (Width and Height Customization)** – Defines precise width and height in pixels for image output.

9. **--seed (Randomization Control)** – Uses a fixed seed number to ensure consistent image outputs for similar prompts. Example: --seed 12345 generates the same image structure every time.

10. **--bw (Black and White Mode)** – Converts the generated image into a monochrome, black-and-white style.

These commands allow users to have greater control over image generation, making Ideogram more flexible for professional and artistic projects.

Here are 10 more Ideogram commands to further refine and customize AI-generated images.

11. --hdr (High Dynamic Range Mode) – Enhances contrast and color vibrancy, making the image appear more vivid and realistic.

12. --sharp (Sharpness Control) – Increases the sharpness and clarity of details in the image, useful for fine textures and intricate designs.

13. --blur (Soft Focus Effect) – Adds a slight blur to soften edges and create a dreamy, cinematic effect.

14. --cam (Camera Perspective Control) – Adjusts the camera angle and depth, allowing you to specify perspectives like "wide-angle," "macro shot," or "close-up."

15. --light (Lighting Adjustment) – Controls the intensity and direction of lighting in the image, useful for dramatic or moody effects.

16. --contrast (Contrast Boost) – Enhances contrast levels, making highlights brighter and shadows deeper for a more dynamic look.

17. --sat (Saturation Control) – Increases or decreases the intensity of colors in the image, making it more vibrant or muted.

18. --motion (Motion Blur Effect) – Simulates movement within the image, creating a dynamic, action-oriented scene.

19. --grain (Film Grain Effect) – Adds a subtle grainy texture for a vintage, cinematic, or retro aesthetic.

20. --glow (Glow Effect) – Adds a soft or intense glow around elements, useful for neon lighting, sci-fi, and fantasy effects.

These additional commands allow for even greater control over the style, lighting, and realism of images in **Ideogram**, making them more **cinematic, artistic, or dramatic** depending on your needs.

Here are **10 more advanced Ideogram commands** to further refine and enhance AI-generated images.

21. --bg (Background Customization) – Allows you to specify the type of background, such as --bg solid black, --bg blurred, or --bg transparent.

22. --depth (Depth Mapping) – Enhances the depth of field effect, making foreground elements stand out while the background appears more distant or blurred.

23. --ambient (Ambient Light Control) – Adjusts the ambient lighting in the image to create soft, evenly spread illumination. Example: --ambient warm glow.

24. --reflect (Reflection Effect) – Adds realistic reflections on surfaces such as glass, water, or metal. Example: --reflect high increases the effect.

25. --outline (Edge Definition) – Enhances the outline of objects for a sharper or more stylized appearance.

26. --metallic (Metallic Texture Boost) – Enhances the metallic sheen on surfaces, making them appear more reflective and realistic.

27. --symmetry (Symmetrical Image Generation) – Forces symmetrical balance in the image composition, useful for portraits, logos, and abstract art.

28. --fog (Atmospheric Fog Effect) – Adds fog or mist to the image, creating a sense of mystery, depth, or cinematic atmosphere.

29. --halftone (Comic Book/Graphic Print Effect) – Applies a halftone shading pattern to make images look like comic book or printed graphics.

30. --neon (Glowing Neon Effect) – Intensifies neon glow effects, ideal for cyberpunk, sci-fi, or retro-futuristic aesthetics.

These commands provide more control over **lighting, reflections, depth, symmetry, and textures**, allowing users to create highly **polished, stylized, or dramatic** visuals in **Ideogram**.

Best Practices for Using Ideogram

To create high-quality AI images, start with a clear objective to ensure the AI understands what you are trying to generate. Using specific contextual details such as colors, lighting, and composition leads to more refined outputs. Requesting multiple versions of an image allows for comparisons and selection of the best result.

Experimentation is key to achieving the best results. Adjust prompts slightly and compare different outputs to see which variations work best for your artistic goals.

AI-generated images can be refined further using editing tools. While Ideogram produces high-quality results, minor touch-ups using Photoshop or other image editing software can enhance the final output.

Final Thoughts

Ideogram is a powerful tool for generating visually stunning AI images across different artistic styles and themes. By crafting detailed and structured prompts, experimenting with styles and lighting, and refining the AI-generated results, users can create unique and high-quality artwork for various purposes.

Whether creating professional graphics, fantasy landscapes, character portraits, or promotional images, Ideogram provides an intuitive and effective way to bring creative visions to life. Experiment with different prompts and styles to fully explore the potential of AI-generated art.

Chapter Six

Canva Tutorial: A Complete Guide to Designing Like a Pro

Introduction to Canva

Canva is a powerful and user-friendly design tool that allows users to create stunning graphics, presentations, social media posts, marketing materials, and much more. Whether you're a beginner or an experienced designer, Canva provides an intuitive interface, pre-made templates, and advanced customization options to help you create visually appealing content effortlessly.

This tutorial will guide you through the basics of using Canva, from setting up an account to utilizing templates and designing from scratch.

Getting Started with Canva

1. Creating an Account

To start using Canva, follow these steps:

1. Visit Canva's website.

2. Click on **Sign up** and choose to register using an email, Google, or Facebook account.

3. Once registered, log in and you will be taken to the Canva dashboard.

2. Navigating the Dashboard

The Canva dashboard includes:

- **Home**: Browse templates and recent projects.

- **Templates**: Access thousands of free and premium templates.

- **Projects**: Find all your saved designs.

- **Brand Kit**: Customize fonts, colors, and logos (Pro feature).

- **Apps & Integrations**: Connect Canva with third-party

tools.

Using Canva Templates

One of Canva's standout features is its extensive template library. Templates provide pre-designed layouts that can be customized to fit your needs.

3. Choosing a Template

1. Click on **Templates** from the dashboard.

2. Use the search bar to find specific templates (e.g., "Instagram Post," "Presentation," "Business Card").

3. Select a template that suits your needs.

4. Customizing a Template

Once you've chosen a template, you can modify it:

- **Text**: Click on any text box to edit the text.

- **Fonts**: Change font style, size, and color from the toolbar.

- **Images**: Replace template images with your own or use Canva's free images.

- **Elements**: Add shapes, lines, stickers, or illustrations.

- **Colors**: Customize colors to match your brand.

Designing from Scratch

If you want to create a unique design without using a template, follow these steps:

5. Starting a New Design

1. Click on **Create a design** in the upper-right corner.

2. Select a predefined size (e.g., Instagram post: 1080x1080px) or enter custom dimensions.

6. Adding Elements to Your Design

1. Click **Elements** to add shapes, lines, and icons.

2. Use the **Text** tab to insert text boxes with predefined styles.

3. Upload your own images under the **Uploads** tab.

4. Drag and resize elements as needed.

7. Adjusting Layers and Positioning

- Right-click on an element to **bring forward** or **send backward**.

- Use the **Position** tool to align objects.

- Group multiple elements together to move them as a unit.

Enhancing Your Design

Canva offers various features to take your design to the next level:

8. Using AI-Powered Features

Canva incorporates artificial intelligence (AI) to simplify and enhance the design process:

- **Magic Write**: An AI-powered text generator for quick content creation.

- **Background Remover**: AI-driven tool to remove backgrounds from images.

- **Text-to-Image**: AI-generated images based on textual descriptions.

- **Design Suggestions**: AI-driven recommendations for layouts and elements.

9. Using Filters and Effects

- Click on an image and select **Edit Image** to apply filters.

- Use effects like **Background Remover** (Pro feature) to enhance visuals.

- Adjust brightness, contrast, and saturation manually.

10. Adding Animations

- Click **Animate** in the top menu to add motion effects.

- Choose from animations like **Fade, Pan, Rise, and Tumble**.

- Use animated elements for social media posts or presentations.

Saving and Exporting Your Design

11. Downloading Your Design

1. Click the **Share** button in the top-right corner.

2. Select **Download** and choose the preferred file format:

   ○ **PNG**: Best for high-quality images.

   ○ **JPG**: Smaller file size with decent quality.

   ○ **PDF**: Ideal for print materials.

   ○ **MP4/GIF**: For animated designs.

3. Click **Download** to save your design to your device.

12. Sharing Your Design

- Share directly via email or link.

- Post on social media platforms like Facebook, Instagram, or Twitter.

- Use **Canva Print** to order physical copies of your design.

Unleashing Your Creativity with Magic Media

Canva's Magic Media is a powerful tool that uses AI to generate images and videos from text prompts. This tutorial will guide you through the process, helping you bring your creative visions to life.

Part 1: Accessing Magic Media

1. **Open Canva:** Launch Canva in your web browser or open the Canva app.

2. **Create a Design:** Choose any design type (e.g., social media post, presentation, flyer). You can start with a blank canvas or select a template.

3. **Find Magic Media:** In the left-hand menu, look for the "Apps" tab. Click it, and search for "Magic Media." Select it to open the Magic Media panel.

Part 2: Generating Images with Magic Media

1. **Enter Your Prompt:** In the text box within the Magic Media panel, describe the image you want to create. Be as specific as possible! The more details you provide, the better the results. For example, instead of "a dog," try "a golden retriev-

er puppy playing fetch in a sunny park." Consider adding artistic styles like "photorealistic," "painting," or "cartoon" to influence the image.

2. **Generate:** Click the "Generate" button. Canva's AI will process your prompt and create several image variations.

3. **Review and Select:** Browse the generated images. If you don't see what you're looking for, you can refine your prompt and generate again. You can also choose a slightly different variation of your original prompt to see what other options are available.

4. **Add to Design:** Once you've found an image you like, click it to add it to your design.

5. **Edit and Adjust:** Just like any other element in Canva, you can resize, reposition, and edit the generated image. You can also apply filters, adjust brightness and contrast, and make other modifications.

Part 3: Generating Videos with Magic Media (currently in beta/preview)

Note: The video generation feature of Magic Media is often in beta or preview, so the interface and functionality might change.

1. **Access Video Generation:** Similar to image generation, ensure you are in the Magic Media section of the Apps tab. There should be a toggle or separate section for Video.

2. **Enter Your Prompt:** Describe the video you want to create. Be very descriptive about the scene, characters, actions, and mood. For example, "A majestic eagle soaring over

snow-capped mountains at sunrise, with dramatic orchestral music."

3. **Generate:** Click the "Generate" button. Canva's AI will process your prompt and create a short video clip.

4. **Review and Select:** Preview the generated video. If you're not happy with the result, refine your prompt and generate again. Experiment with different prompts to achieve the desired outcome.

5. **Add to Design:** Click the video to add it to your design. You can then trim the video, add other elements, and apply effects.

6. **Customize:** You may be able to customize the video further, depending on the current features of Magic Media's video generation. This might include changing the music, adding text overlays, or adjusting the pacing.

Part 4: Tips for Best Results

- **Be Specific:** The more details you provide in your prompt, the better the results will be.

- **Experiment:** Try different prompts and variations to see what works best.

- **Use Keywords:** Include relevant keywords in your prompts to guide the AI.

- **Iterate:** Don't be afraid to regenerate images or videos multiple times until you get the desired outcome.

- **Combine with Other Canva Features:** Use Magic Media in conjunction with Canva's other design tools to create truly unique and stunning visuals.

- **Check for Updates:** Magic Media is constantly evolving, so keep an eye out for new features and improvements.

Part 5: Troubleshooting

- **Slow Generation:** Generating images and videos can take some time, especially for complex prompts. Be patient.

- **Unexpected Results:** AI is still under development, so sometimes the results might not be exactly what you expected. Refine your prompt and try again.

- **Limited Functionality:** The video generation feature is often in beta. Be aware of its limitations and expect changes.

By following this tutorial, you'll be well on your way to mastering Canva's Magic Media and creating amazing visuals for all your projects. Have fun exploring its creative potential!

Five Sample Magic Media Prompts You Can Build On

1. **Product Demo Video:** A dynamic video showcasing a new noise-canceling headphone, highlighting its features like crystal-clear audio, comfortable design, and long battery life, with upbeat music and sleek visuals. Focus on lifestyle shots of people using the headphones in different scenarios.

2. **Social Media Ad for a Fitness App:** A short, motivational video ad for a fitness app, featuring diverse individuals working out

and achieving their fitness goals, with energetic music and text overlays highlighting the app's key features and a clear call to action ("Download Now").

3. Explainer Video for SaaS Product: A concise and engaging animated explainer video for a project management SaaS platform, illustrating how it simplifies workflows, improves team collaboration, and boosts productivity, using clear visuals and a friendly voiceover.

4. Customer Testimonial Video: A heartwarming video featuring a satisfied customer sharing their success story using a meal delivery service, showcasing the convenience, healthy options, and positive impact it has had on their life, with genuine testimonials and relatable visuals.

5. Brand Story Video: A visually stunning video showcasing the history and values of a sustainable clothing brand, highlighting their commitment to ethical sourcing, eco-friendly materials, and positive social impact, with inspiring music and authentic footage of their production process.

Six Magic Media Prompts to Generate Business Related Images

Here are 6 Magic Media prompts geared towards sales and marketing visuals, covering logos, office workers, and headshots:

1. Modern Logo Design

A sleek and minimalist logo design incorporating abstract shapes and vibrant gradients, conveying innovation and forward-thinking for a tech startup.

2. Dynamic Team Collaboration

Realistic, photo quality office workers collaborating energetically around a table, brainstorming ideas with animated gestures and focused expressions, showcasing teamwork and creativity.

3. Professional Headshot

A confident and approachable headshot of a business professional, with a warm smile and a professional yet friendly background, emphasizing trustworthiness and expertise.

4. Social Media Ad Graphic

An eye-catching graphic for a social media ad campaign, featuring a special offer or promotion with clear call-to-action buttons and visually appealing typography.

5. Website Banner Design

A captivating website banner design for an e-commerce store, promoting a seasonal sale with attractive product images and a clear call to action.

6. Business Card Design

A modern and professional business card design, incorporating the company logo and contact information in a clean and memorable layout.

Exploring Canva Pro Features

While Canva's free version is powerful, Canva Pro offers additional features:

- **Brand Kit**: Save brand colors, fonts, and logos.

- **Magic Resize**: Instantly adjust design dimensions.

- **Background Remover**: Remove image backgrounds with one click.

- **Premium Templates & Elements**: Access exclusive design resources.

- **Collaboration Tools**: Work on designs with a team.

Tips and Tricks for Better Designs

1. **Use Consistent Fonts & Colors**: Maintain uniformity in design.

2. **Utilize Grid & Alignment Tools**: Ensure elements are perfectly placed.

3. **Keep It Simple**: Avoid overcrowding your design with too many elements.

4. **Experiment with Transparency**: Create depth by adjusting element opacity.

5. **Incorporate Icons & Illustrations**: Enhance visual appeal with Canva's extensive library.

Conclusion

Canva is an incredibly versatile tool that makes designing accessible to everyone, regardless of experience level. With its vast selection of templates, customization options, and AI-powered features, you can create professional-quality designs in minutes. Whether you're designing for personal use, business branding, or social media, Canva provides all the tools you need.

Now that you have a solid understanding of Canva, start exploring, get creative, and design something amazing!

Chapter Seven

Unleash Your Inner Artist: A DALL-E 2 Tutorial for Stunning Business Graphics

D ALL-E 2, OpenAI's revolutionary AI image generator, empowers you to create breathtaking visuals from simple text descriptions. This tutorial will guide you through the basics of DALL-E 2, focusing on generating stunning graphics for your business, including logos, web marketing ads, and more. We'll also explore the powerful image editing capabilities, including the regular edit feature.

What is DALL-E 2?

DALL-E 2 is an AI system that generates realistic and creative images from natural language descriptions, called "prompts." You provide the text, and DALL-E 2 interprets it, producing unique visuals. It's a powerful tool for brainstorming, prototyping, and creating final artwork.

Getting Started:

1. **Access:** You'll need access to DALL-E 2. While initially invite-only, access is becoming increasingly available. Check OpenAI's website for the latest information.

2. **The Prompt is Key:** The quality of your generated image hinges on the clarity and detail of your prompt. Think of it as giving precise instructions to a human artist.

3. **Iteration is Your Friend:** Don't expect perfection from the first try. Experiment with different prompts, variations, and edits to refine your results.

Crafting Effective Prompts:

A good prompt is specific, descriptive, and imaginative. Consider these elements:

- **Subject:** What is the main focus of the image? (e.g., "a logo," "a website banner," "a social media post")

- **Style:** What artistic style do you want? (e.g., "minimalist," "abstract," "photorealistic," "watercolor," "pop art")

- **Composition:** How should the elements be arranged? (e.g., "close-up," "wide shot," "centered," "diagonal")

- **Color Palette:** What colors should be dominant? (e.g., "vibrant," "pastel," "monochromatic," "red and blue")

- **Mood/Atmosphere:** What feeling should the image evoke? (e.g., "professional," "playful," "serious," "exciting")

- **Specific Details:** The more details you provide, the better DALL-E 2 can understand your vision. (e.g., "with geometric shapes," "with a futuristic background," "featuring a smiling person")

Using DALL-E 2's Features:

- **Image Generation:** Simply type your prompt into the text box and let DALL-E 2 work its magic.

- **Variations:** Once you have a good image, you can generate variations to explore different options.

- **Edits (Including Inpainting and the Regular Edit Feature):** DALL-E 2 offers two main ways to edit images:

  - **Inpainting:** This allows you to select a specific area of an image and regenerate it based on a new prompt. It's ideal for adding, removing, or significantly altering parts of the image.

  - **Regular Edit:** This feature allows you to upload your own image or use a previously generated one and then provide a prompt describing how you want to modify the *entire* image. DALL-E 2 will attempt to make changes while preserving the existing style and overall composition. This is excellent for broader changes like adjusting lighting, adding a background, or changing the overall theme.

- **Upscaling:** Improve the resolution of your generated images for higher-quality output.

Editing Images with DALL-E 2 (Regular Edit):

1. **Upload or Select an Image:** You can either upload your own image or choose one you've already generated in DALL-E 2.

2. **Describe the Change:** Enter a prompt describing the modification you want to make to the *entire* image. For example, if you have a product photo on a white background and want to place it on a wooden table, your prompt might be: "A product photo on a rustic wooden table."

3. **Maintaining Style During Edits:** This is crucial for consistent branding. Try to preserve the existing style by referencing elements like "same product," "original lighting," "similar composition," or specific colors in your prompt. Example: "The same product photo, now on a rustic wooden table, maintaining the original lighting and perspective." This helps DALL-E 2 understand that you want to keep the core elements of the image intact while changing the background.

Editing Images with DALL-E 2 (Inpainting): See the previous response for details on using the inpainting feature.

10 Example Prompts for Business Graphics (Including Regular and Inpainting Edits)

1. **Logo:** "A minimalist logo for a tech startup, featuring a stylized circuit board, in a clean sans-serif font, using a color palette of blue and white." *Regular Edit: "The same logo, now with a subtle glow effect." Inpainting Edit: Select the text and prompt: "The same logo, but with the text in a bold, futuristic sans-serif font."*

2. **Website Banner:** "A vibrant website banner for a travel agency, showcasing a tropical beach at sunset, with the text 'Book Your Dream Vacation' in a bold, modern font."

3. **Social Media Post:** "A playful social media post for a coffee shop, featuring a cartoon illustration of a steaming cup of coffee, with the text 'Wake Up and Smell the Coffee!' in a handwritten font."

4. **Product Packaging:** "Photorealistic image of product packaging for organic honey, featuring a honeycomb pattern and a vintage-style label, with the text 'Pure Honey' in a classic serif font."

5. **Infographic:** "An infographic illustrating the benefits of using cloud computing, with icons representing data storage, security, and accessibility, using a clean and modern design."

6. **Business Card:** "A professional business card design for a

graphic designer, featuring a geometric pattern and the contact information in a sleek, minimalist font, using a color scheme of black and white."

7. **Marketing Ad:** "A dynamic marketing ad for a fitness app, featuring a person running on a treadmill with a futuristic cityscape in the background, with the text 'Achieve Your Fitness Goals' in a bold, energetic font." *Regular Edit: "The same ad, but with the cityscape at night."*

8. **Presentation Slide:** "A visually appealing presentation slide for a sales pitch, featuring a graph showing sales growth, with a clean and professional design, using a color palette of green and white."

9. **Blog Post Image:** "An eye-catching image for a blog post about sustainable living, featuring a lush green forest with a clear blue sky, with the text 'Go Green' in a natural, earthy font."

10. **App Icon:** "A simple and memorable app icon for a language learning app, featuring a stylized speech bubble, using a vibrant color palette and a modern, geometric design." *Inpainting Edit: Select the speech bubble and prompt: "The same icon, but with the speech bubble redesigned as a stylized open book."*

Tips for Success

- **Be Specific:** The more specific you are, the better the results.

- **Experiment:** Don't be afraid to try different prompts and variations.

- **Iterate:** Refine your prompts based on the results you get.

- **Use References:** If you have a specific style in mind, reference it in your prompt.

- **Combine Prompts:** You can combine multiple prompts to create complex images.

- **Maintain Style During Edits:** Use language that connects the edit back to the original image to preserve consistency. Distinguish between the *inpainting* edits (for localized changes) and *regular* edits (for whole image changes).

DALL-E 2 is a powerful tool for generating stunning business graphics. By mastering the art of prompt engineering and leveraging the edit features, you can unlock its full potential and create visuals that will elevate your brand and marketing efforts. Start experimenting, and unleash your creativity!

Chapter Eight

MidJourney Tutorial: How to Create Stunning AI-Generated Images

Introduction to MidJourney

MidJourney is a powerful AI-driven image generation tool that allows users to create stunning visuals from simple text prompts. It is widely used by artists, designers, and enthusiasts who want to bring their creative visions to life with minimal effort. Whether you are looking to create fantasy landscapes, sci-fi scenes, serene seashores, or realistic images of people in everyday settings, MidJourney can help you generate high-quality artwork in seconds.

In this tutorial, you'll learn how to use MidJourney effectively and explore 10 sample prompts to create breathtaking images in different categories.

Getting Started with MidJourney

Step 1: Access MidJourney

MidJourney is now available as a standalone web application, eliminating the need for Discord. To start using it:

1. Visit the MidJourney website.

2. Sign up or log in to your account.

3. Subscribe to a MidJourney plan to gain access to the image generation features.

Step 2: Use the Prompt System

Once inside the MidJourney web app:

1. Locate the prompt input field.

2. Type a descriptive text prompt for the image you want to generate.

3. Press the generate button, and MidJourney will create four variations of the image based on your description.

4. Use the available options to upscale or refine your chosen image.

Step 3: Adjust Settings for Better Results

- **Aspect Ratio:** Use --ar to adjust width and height (e.g., --ar 16:9 for widescreen images).

- **Quality:** Use --q to set quality (higher values use more processing time, e.g., --q 2).

- **Style:** Use --s to adjust artistic style (e.g., --s 500 for a highly detailed image).

- **Version:** Use --v to specify which version of MidJourney's AI you want to use.

Now that you know the basics, let's explore 10 sample prompts!

10 Sample MidJourney Prompts

1. Fantasy Landscape

"A majestic floating island with cascading waterfalls, lush green forests, and ancient ruins glowing with magical runes, ethereal mist in the background, cinematic lighting --ar 16:9 --q 2 --s 500 --v 5"

This prompt will generate a breathtaking fantasy environment perfect for storytelling or concept art.

2. Sci-Fi Cityscape

"A futuristic cyberpunk city with neon-lit skyscrapers, flying cars, bustling streets filled with humanoid robots and people wearing cybernetic enhancements, dramatic lighting, ultra-detailed --ar 16:9 --q 2 --s 750 --v 5"

This prompt will produce an intense, high-tech cityscape with strong sci-fi aesthetics.

3. Majestic Mountain Range

"A stunning snow-capped mountain range with golden sunlight illuminating the peaks, a peaceful valley below with a winding river, dramatic clouds, ultra-realistic --ar 16:9 --q 2 --s 500 --v 5"

This is great for creating breathtaking nature photography-style images.

4. Serene Seashore at Sunset

"A tranquil seashore with soft golden sand, gentle waves crashing against rocky cliffs, a lighthouse glowing in the distance, pink and orange sunset hues reflecting on the water, dreamy atmosphere --ar 16:9 --q 2 --s 600 --v 5"

A perfect prompt for capturing the beauty and peace of the ocean.

5. People in a Park on a Sunny Day

"A lively city park with people jogging, children playing, families having picnics, tall green trees providing shade, bright sunny day, ultra-realistic photography style --ar 16:9 --q 2 --s 400 --v 5"

This will generate an image that feels warm, inviting, and full of life.

6. Family Walking Down a New York City Street

"A young family walking down a bustling New York City street, parents pushing a stroller with a baby, tall skyscrapers, yellow cabs, pedestrians, realistic lighting, urban energy, detailed architecture --ar 16:9 --q 2 --s 700 --v 5"

A fantastic way to capture everyday city life with high realism.

7. Mystical Forest with Hidden Secrets

"A dense mystical forest with ancient towering trees, glowing fireflies, an enchanted pathway leading to an old wooden bridge, soft magical mist, dreamlike lighting --ar 16:9 --q 2 --s 600 --v 5"

This prompt creates a fantasy forest scene ideal for fairytales or magical storytelling.

8. Dystopian Post-Apocalyptic Ruins

"A desolate post-apocalyptic city overgrown with nature, abandoned skyscrapers covered in vines, rusted vehicles, a lone survivor with a gas mask walking through, moody and cinematic --ar 16:9 --q 2 --s 750 --v 5 "

This generates a haunting yet visually stunning dystopian environment.

9. Epic Battle Scene

"A massive battle between armored knights and fire-breathing drag-
ons, dust and smoke rising, intense action, cinematic lighting, dynamic composition, ultra-detailed fantasy art --ar 16:9 --q 2 --s 800 --v 5"

This will create an action-packed fantasy battle scene with high
visual impact.

10. Cozy Winter Cabin in the Mountains

"A warm and cozy wooden cabin in a snowy mountain landscape, soft
glowing lights from the windows, smoke rising from the chimney, tall
evergreen trees covered in snow, peaceful night sky with twinkling stars
--ar 16:9 --q 2 --s 600 --v 5"

This prompt generates a picturesque and comforting winter scene.

Conclusion

MidJourney is a powerful tool for creating beautiful AI-generated
images. By using descriptive prompts and adjusting parameters like aspect ratio, quality, and style, you can fine-tune your results for incredible artwork. Whether you are interested in fantasy, sci-fi, nature, or
everyday realism, MidJourney provides endless creative possibilities.

Try experimenting with different prompts and parameters to unlock your unique artistic style. Happy generating!

Help Others with Your Review

Make AI Easy for Everyone

"A little help goes a long way." - Anonymous

The best way to learn is by sharing what we know. When we take a moment to help someone else, we make the world a little better—not just for them, but for ourselves too.

So, I have a question for you...

Would you help a stranger if it cost you nothing?

This person is like you—curious about AI, eager to understand it, but maybe not sure where to start. They want to use AI to make life easier, work smarter, and stay ahead in a fast-changing world.

That's why *The AI Handbook for Everyone* exists—to make AI simple, clear, and useful for everyday people. But to reach more readers, we need your help.

A quick review of the book—just a few words about what you liked—can help someone decide to take that first step into AI.

Review Link – https://www.amazon.com/review/create-review/?ie=UTF8&channel=glance-detail&asin=B0DXSH3Y4J

If this book has helped you, inspired you, or made AI a little less confusing, your review can do the same for someone else.

And that's how we grow together.

Thank you for being part of this journey.

Chapter Nine

---

100 ChatGPT Prompts for Everyday Use

Top 10 Tasks On ChatGPT

C hatGPT has become a versatile tool for users across various domains, assisting with a wide range of tasks. Based on user reports and studies, here are the top 10 activities consumers frequently utilize ChatGPT for:

1. **Writing Extended Prose**: Users employ ChatGPT to draft essays, articles, and other long-form content, benefiting from its ability to generate coherent and contextually relevant text.

2. **Composing Emails and Letters**: The AI assists in crafting professional and personal correspondence, ensuring clarity

and appropriate tone.

3. **Creative Writing**: From poetry to storytelling, users leverage ChatGPT's creative capabilities to brainstorm ideas and develop narratives.

4. **Social Media Content Creation**: ChatGPT aids in generating engaging posts and captions tailored for various social media platforms.

5. **Academic Assistance**: Students utilize ChatGPT for explanations of complex concepts, drafting essays, and solving problems, making it a valuable educational tool.

6. **Translation Services**: The AI provides translations between languages, helping users understand and communicate across linguistic barriers.

7. **Job Application Support**: Job seekers use ChatGPT to write and refine résumés and cover letters, enhancing their professional profiles.

8. **Coding and Programming Help**: Developers turn to ChatGPT for writing code snippets, debugging, and understanding programming concepts.

9. **Idea Generation and Brainstorming**: Users seek ChatGPT's assistance in generating ideas for projects, content, and problem-solving scenarios.

10. **Personalized Recommendations**: ChatGPT offers tailored suggestions for books, movies, travel destinations, and more, based on user preferences.

These activities can be categorized into the following top 10 domains:

1. **Content Creation**: Encompasses writing articles, essays, and creative pieces.

2. **Communication**: Involves drafting emails, letters, and social media content.

3. **Education**: Includes academic assistance, explanations, and learning support.

4. **Programming**: Covers coding help, debugging, and code generation.

5. **Translation**: Pertains to converting text between languages.

6. **Professional Development**: Focuses on job applications, résumé building, and cover letter writing.

7. **Creative Arts**: Relates to poetry, storytelling, and other artistic endeavors.

8. **Idea Generation**: Involves brainstorming and developing new concepts.

9. **Personal Assistance**: Offers recommendations and planning for personal activities.

10. **Social Interaction**: Assists with composing messages and improving interpersonal communications.

100 ChatGPT Prompts for Everyday Use

These categories highlight the diverse applications of ChatGPT, reflecting its integration into both personal and professional aspects of users' lives.

Writing Prose

1. **Personal Journal Entry**

   "I want to write a personal journal entry reflecting on my day. My main activities included [describe your day], and I felt [describe emotions]. Please write a thoughtful and engaging journal entry in the first person, capturing my thoughts and feelings. Keep it introspective yet conversational."

2. **Storytelling for Kids**

   "I need to tell a bedtime story to a [age] year-old child about a brave [animal or character] who embarks on an adventure in a magical land. The story should be engaging, age-appropriate, and include a moral lesson about [kindness, bravery, honesty, etc.]. Please write a short, imaginative story with dialogue."

3. **Reflective Letter to My Future Self**

   "I'd like to write a letter to my future self, one year from today. In this letter, I want to reflect on my current struggles, dreams, and goals. I also want to include words of encouragement, reminders of important values, and a few questions to reflect on. Please write this letter in a warm and inspiring tone."

4. **Captivating Social Media Post**

   "I want to create an engaging social media post about [topic—travel, food, productivity, self-care, etc.]. The post should

have a compelling hook, a relatable story, and a call to action that encourages engagement (e.g., asking followers for their experiences). Please make it conversational and engaging, suitable for Instagram/Facebook."

5. **Personal Essay for Self-Improvement**

"I am reflecting on an important life lesson I recently learned: [describe lesson]. I'd like to turn this into a personal essay that tells a short anecdote, explains the lesson learned, and provides insights that others might find valuable. Please make it engaging and thought-provoking, around 500 words."

6. **Motivational Speech for a Small Audience**

"I need to give a short motivational speech to a small group of friends or colleagues about overcoming challenges. The speech should start with a personal anecdote, introduce a universal lesson, and end with an inspiring call to action. Please write this in a passionate yet conversational tone, around 3-5 minutes long."

7. **Wedding or Special Occasion Toast**

"I have to give a toast at [wedding, birthday, retirement, anniversary, etc.]. The toast should be heartfelt, a little humorous, and express my deep appreciation for [person's name]. Include a personal story, a warm message, and a memorable closing. Please make it lighthearted and sincere."

8. **Engaging Travel Blog Post**

"I recently visited [destination] and want to write a travel blog post about my experience. The post should include a vivid description of the location, highlights of the trip, cultural insights,

and practical tips for future travelers. Please make it engaging, informative, and immersive."

9. **Thought-Provoking Opinion Piece**

   "I'd like to write an opinion piece on [current event, social issue, lifestyle trend, etc.]. It should present a clear argument, provide supporting evidence or examples, and invite discussion. Please write it in a compelling and well-structured way, with a strong introduction and conclusion."

10. **Heartfelt Thank You Letter**

    "I want to write a thank-you letter to [someone important—teacher, mentor, friend, family member] who has made a difference in my life. The letter should express my deep gratitude, include specific examples of their impact, and be warm and personal. Please write this in a sincere and appreciative tone."

Composing Emails and Letters

1. **Professional Email Request**

   "I need to write a professional email requesting [specific request] from [recipient]. The email should be clear, concise, and polite, with a strong subject line and a call to action. Please structure it professionally while maintaining a warm and respectful tone."

2. **Follow-Up Email After a Meeting**

   "I recently had a meeting with [person or company], and I want to send a follow-up email summarizing key points, ex-

pressing gratitude, and outlining next steps. Please craft a professional yet friendly email that reinforces our discussion and encourages continued engagement."

3. Apology Letter for a Mistake

"I need to write an apology letter to [recipient] for [describe mistake]. The letter should express sincere regret, take responsibility, and offer a solution or plan to prevent future issues. Please make it professional yet empathetic."

4. Job Application Cover Letter

"I'm applying for a [job title] position at [company name]. My key qualifications include [list relevant skills/experience]. Please write a compelling cover letter that highlights my strengths, aligns with the job description, and conveys enthusiasm for the role."

5. Resignation Letter

"I am resigning from my position at [company name] as [job title], effective [date]. I'd like to express gratitude for my time at the company while maintaining professionalism. Please write a polite and appreciative resignation letter that leaves a positive impression."

6. Networking Email for Career Opportunities

"I want to reach out to [recipient] to explore potential career opportunities and seek advice. Please draft a professional and engaging email that introduces myself, expresses admiration for their work, and politely requests a conversation or mentorship."

7. Letter of Recommendation

"I am writing a letter of recommendation for [name] for [job, school, award, etc.]. They have demonstrated [list qualities, skills, and achievements]. Please write a compelling and detailed letter that highlights their strengths and qualifications."

8. Customer Complaint Email

"I need to write a formal complaint email to [company] about [issue with product/service]. The email should be firm but polite, clearly explaining the problem, requesting a resolution, and providing necessary details. Please make it professional and solution-oriented."

9. Holiday or Thank You Card Message

"I want to write a heartfelt holiday/thank you message to [recipient]. The message should be warm, personal, and appreciative, expressing gratitude for their kindness, support, or friendship. Please make it meaningful and engaging."

10. Invitation Email for an Event

"I'm hosting [event type] on [date] at [location] and want to invite [recipient/group]. The email should be engaging, provide clear event details, and include an RSVP request. Please make it friendly yet professional, suitable for the audience."

Creative Writing

1. Short Story Prompt

"I want to write a short story about [theme or idea]. The story should include a compelling protagonist, a clear conflict, and a satisfying resolution. Please craft an engaging and imagi-

native story with strong character development and vivid de-
scriptions."

2. Poem on a Personal Experience

"I'd like to write a poem about [specific experience, emotion, or
theme]. The poem should be expressive, thought-provoking, and
use vivid imagery. Please write it in a style that conveys deep
emotion, whether free verse, rhyming, or haiku, based on the
theme."

3. Dialogue Between Two Characters

"I need to write a realistic and engaging dialogue between two
characters discussing [topic]. One character is [describe person-
ality], and the other is [describe personality]. The conversation
should feel natural, reveal character traits, and create tension
or resolution."

4. Fantasy World-Building Description

"I am creating a fantasy world with unique landscapes, cul-
tures, and magic systems. Please write a detailed description
of this world, including geography, society, and any mystical
elements, making it immersive and vivid for storytelling."

5. Mystery Story Opening Scene

"I need an intriguing opening scene for a mystery story. The
scene should introduce the main character, hint at the central
mystery, and set a suspenseful tone. Please write a compelling
beginning that immediately hooks the reader."

6. Letter from One Fictional Character to Another

"I want to write a letter from [fictional character] to [another
fictional character] about [situation]. The letter should reflect

the character's voice, emotions, and relationship with the recipient. Please make it engaging and authentic to the character's personality."

7. **Science Fiction Story Concept**

"I'd like to develop a science fiction story set in the year [future date]. The plot should involve [main theme, e.g., AI, space travel, dystopian society]. Please create a unique concept with an engaging premise and world-building elements."

8. **Comedic Scene with Witty Banter**

"I need a humorous scene where two characters engage in witty banter about [topic]. The humor should be lighthearted and engaging, with a playful back-and-forth dynamic. Please write the dialogue in a way that makes the scene fun and memorable."

9. **Character Backstory Development**

"I want to create a backstory for my character, [name]. They are [age, personality, background]. Please write a compelling character history that explains their motivations, struggles, and key life events that shaped who they are."

10. **Dramatic Monologue for a Play or Story**

"I need a powerful monologue for a character facing [internal conflict]. The speech should be emotionally charged, revealing deep personal struggles and growth. Please write it in a way that feels authentic and moving for an audience."

Social Media Content Creation

1. Engaging Instagram Caption

"I want to write an engaging Instagram caption for a post about [topic—travel, food, fitness, motivation, etc.]. The caption should include a compelling hook, a personal touch, and a call to action to encourage comments. Please keep it concise and impactful."

2. Inspirational Twitter/X Post

"I need a short but powerful Twitter/X post about [theme—motivation, success, mindfulness, etc.]. It should be under 280 characters, include a thought-provoking message, and encourage engagement through a question or call to action."

3. LinkedIn Post on Professional Growth

"I want to write a LinkedIn post sharing insights on [professional topic—career growth, leadership, productivity, networking]. The post should include a personal experience, a key lesson, and a question to encourage discussion. Please make it professional yet relatable."

4. Facebook Post About a Personal Achievement

"I want to share a Facebook post about a recent achievement in [career, fitness, personal life]. The post should be uplifting, share the journey behind the success, and inspire others to reflect on their own goals. Please make it engaging and heartfelt."

5. TikTok/YouTube Video Script for Storytelling

"I need a short script for a TikTok or YouTube video where I tell a story about [topic—funny moment, life lesson, travel experience, etc.]. The script should have a captivating opening, a

relatable middle, and a strong ending that leaves an impact."

6. **Engaging Poll or Question for Audience Engagement**

   "I want to create an interactive social media post that encourages my followers to engage. It should be a thought-provoking question or a fun poll related to [topic]. Please craft a post that sparks curiosity and invites people to comment or vote."

7. **Educational Thread for Twitter/X**

   "I want to create a Twitter/X thread that educates my audience on [topic—tech, history, health, finance, etc.]. The first tweet should have a strong hook, and each following tweet should break down key points in a clear and engaging way. Please structure it for readability and impact."

8. **Behind-the-Scenes Instagram Story Script**

   "I need a script for an Instagram Story where I share behind-the-scenes insights about [project, daily routine, special event]. It should be casual and engaging, encouraging viewers to respond or ask questions. Please keep it conversational and fun."

9. **Product or Service Promotion Post**

   "I am promoting [product or service] on social media and want a post that highlights its benefits in an authentic way. The post should include a personal testimonial, key features, and a subtle call to action. Please make it engaging and not overly sales-focused."

10. **Viral Meme or Trend-Based Post**

    "I want to create a funny and relatable post that aligns with a trending meme or social media trend. The post should connect

to my niche [e.g., tech, fitness, parenting] and be shareable. Please craft a witty caption that makes the content fun and engaging."

Academic Assistance

1. Essay Outline and Structure

"I need help creating an outline for an academic essay on [topic]. The essay should follow a clear structure with an introduction, three main points, and a conclusion. Please provide a detailed outline with key arguments and supporting evidence for each section."

2. Summarizing a Complex Concept

"I need a clear and concise explanation of [complex topic—e.g., quantum mechanics, economic theory, historical event] in simple terms. The explanation should be structured logically and include real-world examples to make it easier to understand."

3. Research Paper Thesis Statement

"I am writing a research paper on [subject] and need a strong, focused thesis statement. The statement should be specific, debatable, and reflect the main argument of my paper. Please provide a few options along with a brief explanation of why they work."

4. Annotated Bibliography Entry

"I am compiling an annotated bibliography for my research on [topic]. Please provide a properly formatted entry for the source

[book, article, or website], including a summary of its main points, its relevance to my research, and its credibility."

5. Mathematical Problem Explanation

"I am struggling to understand how to solve this math problem: [insert problem]. Please explain the step-by-step process in a way that makes it easy to follow, along with the reasoning behind each step."

6. Study Guide for Exam Preparation

"I need a study guide for an upcoming exam on [subject]. The guide should include key concepts, important definitions, and sample questions with answers. Please make it structured and easy to review."

7. Scientific Report Conclusion

"I am writing a scientific report on [experiment or study] and need a strong conclusion. The conclusion should summarize the key findings, discuss their significance, and suggest potential areas for further research."

8. Comparative Analysis of Two Theories

"I need a comparative analysis of [Theory A] and [Theory B] in the field of [subject]. Please outline their key similarities and differences, provide examples of how they are applied, and conclude with an evaluation of which is more effective in a given context."

9. Critical Analysis of a Literary Work

"I am analyzing [book, poem, or play] by [author] and need a critical analysis of its themes, characters, and literary techniques. Please provide an insightful discussion that includes

evidence from the text."

10. Lab Report Discussion Section

"I am writing the discussion section of my lab report on [experiment topic]. The discussion should interpret the results, compare them with expected outcomes, and address any sources of error. Please make it clear, logical, and concise."

Translation Services

1. Everyday Conversation Translation

"Please translate the following everyday conversation from [source language] to [target language]: '[insert text].' Ensure that the translation is natural, culturally appropriate, and suitable for informal spoken dialogue."

2. Professional Email Translation

"I need to translate a professional email from [source language] to [target language]. The email should maintain a formal tone, proper grammar, and cultural appropriateness while keeping the message clear and polite. Here is the text: '[insert email].'"

3. Social Media Post Translation

"I want to post on social media in [target language] about [topic]. Please translate the following message into [target language] while keeping it engaging and culturally relevant: '[insert text].'"

4. Tourist Phrase Guide Translation

"I am traveling to [destination] and need a list of useful

phrases translated from [source language] to [target language]. The phrases should include greetings, ordering food, asking for directions, and emergency situations."

5. **Website Content Translation**

"I need to translate a section of my website from [source language] to [target language]. The translation should be professional, user-friendly, and optimized for readability. Here is the text: '[insert content].'"

6. **Book or Article Excerpt Translation**

"I need to translate a passage from a book or article from [source language] to [target language]. The translation should preserve the tone, meaning, and style of the original text. Here is the passage: '[insert excerpt].'"

7. **Subtitles for a Video**

"I need to create subtitles in [target language] for a video that is in [source language]. The translation should be accurate, natural, and concise to fit within subtitle timing constraints. Here is the transcript: '[insert dialogue].'"

8. **Medical or Legal Document Translation**

"I need a precise and professional translation of a [medical or legal] document from [source language] to [target language]. Please ensure accuracy and proper use of technical terminology while maintaining a formal and official tone. Here is the text: '[insert document].'"

9. **Poem or Song Lyrics Translation**

"Please translate this poem/song from [source language] to [target language] while preserving its rhythm, meaning, and

emotional tone. Feel free to make slight adaptations if necessary for cultural relevance. Here is the text: '[insert lyrics or poem].'"

10. **Instruction Manual Translation**

"I need to translate an instruction manual for [product or process] from [source language] to [target language]. The translation should be clear, precise, and easy to follow. Here is the text: '[insert manual section].'"

Professional Development

1. **Résumé Rewrite and Optimization**

"I need to rewrite my résumé for a job in [industry or role]. Please format it professionally, highlight my key skills and achievements, and ensure it is ATS-friendly. Here is my current résumé: '[insert text or key details].'"

2. **Cover Letter for Job Application**

"I am applying for a [job title] position at [company name]. My experience includes [list relevant skills and accomplishments]. Please write a compelling cover letter that emphasizes my strengths, aligns with the job description, and conveys enthusiasm for the role."

3. **LinkedIn Profile Summary**

"I want to update my LinkedIn profile summary to reflect my expertise in [industry or skill]. The summary should be professional, engaging, and highlight my career achievements while keeping a personal touch. Please keep it under 300 words."

4. Networking Email for Career Growth

"I want to reach out to [professional contact] to explore potential career opportunities or mentorship. Please draft a professional yet friendly networking email that introduces myself, expresses admiration for their work, and politely requests a meeting or conversation."

5. Personal Statement for Graduate School

"I am applying to [graduate program] at [university] and need a strong personal statement. It should highlight my academic background, research interests, and career goals while showing my passion for the field. Please make it compelling and well-structured."

6. Salary Negotiation Email

"I received a job offer from [company name] for the position of [job title]. While I'm excited about the opportunity, I would like to negotiate a higher salary based on my experience and market rates. Please draft a polite and persuasive salary negotiation email."

7. Conference or Public Speaking Proposal

"I want to submit a proposal to speak at [conference/event] on the topic of [subject]. The proposal should clearly outline my expertise, the key takeaways for the audience, and why this topic is valuable. Please write a compelling and professional proposal."

8. Performance Review Self-Assessment

"I need to write a self-assessment for my annual performance review at work. It should highlight my accomplishments, con-

tributions to the team, and areas for growth. Please make it professional, balanced, and results-oriented."

9. **Business Introduction Email**

"I am introducing myself and my business, [business name], to a potential client or partner. The email should be professional, engaging, and clearly explain what my business offers while encouraging further discussion. Please write a strong introduction email."

10. **Career Change Justification Letter**

"I am transitioning from [current career field] to [new career field] and need to explain my motivation and transferable skills in a cover letter or statement. Please craft a persuasive and professional justification that highlights my strengths and adaptability."

Creative Arts

1. **Writing a Song Lyrics Draft**

"I want to write a song about [theme—love, heartbreak, resilience, adventure, etc.]. The lyrics should be emotional and structured with verses, a chorus, and a bridge. Please make it poetic and engaging, fitting the genre of [pop, country, rock, etc.]."

2. **Script for a Short Film or Play Scene**

"I need a script for a short film/play scene about [theme or conflict]. The scene should have strong dialogue, emotional depth, and a clear beginning, middle, and end. Please include

stage directions or camera cues where necessary."

3. Descriptive Painting or Photography Caption

"I have a painting/photograph of [describe artwork], and I need a compelling caption that explains its meaning and evokes emotion in the audience. Please make it poetic and thought-provoking."

4. Artistic Statement for an Exhibition

"I am showcasing my artwork at an exhibition and need an artist's statement. It should describe my artistic style, inspirations, and the message behind my work. Please make it clear, engaging, and professional."

5. Poetry Inspired by a Personal Memory

"I want to write a poem inspired by a memory of [describe memory—childhood, love, loss, etc.]. The poem should be vivid, emotional, and use strong imagery. Please keep it in free verse or rhyming form based on what fits best."

6. Monologue for a Theater Performance

"I need a dramatic monologue for a character who is experiencing [emotion—grief, joy, anger, hope, etc.]. The monologue should be powerful, introspective, and showcase deep character development."

7. Children's Book Story Idea

"I want to write a children's book about [theme—friendship, bravery, kindness, etc.]. The story should be simple, engaging, and have a clear moral lesson. Please provide a brief outline and a sample opening paragraph."

8. Calligraphy or Typography Quote Creation

"I am designing a piece of calligraphy/typography with the phrase '[insert phrase].' I need a visually appealing and inspiring variation of this quote that enhances its meaning. Please provide a few wording or structural variations."

9. Concept for a Visual Art Piece

"I am creating an art piece based on [theme—identity, nature, technology, etc.]. I need a detailed description of a unique concept that would translate well into a painting, sculpture, or digital artwork."

10. Stand-Up Comedy Routine or Sketch

"I want to write a short stand-up comedy routine or a sketch about [topic—daily life, relationships, technology, etc.]. The jokes should be witty, relatable, and structured to build up to a strong punchline."

Idea Generation

1. Brainstorming Business Ideas

"I want to start a business in [industry or niche], but I need help brainstorming unique and profitable ideas. Please generate a list of creative business concepts, considering current trends and potential market demand."

2. Content Ideas for a Blog or YouTube Channel

"I run a blog/YouTube channel about [topic—tech, travel, fitness, personal development, etc.]. Please generate a list of engaging content ideas that would attract an audience and en-

courage interaction."

3. Innovative Product or App Idea

"I want to create a new product or mobile app that solves a common problem in [industry]. Please brainstorm unique and practical ideas that could be turned into a viable business."

4. Book or Novel Concept

"I want to write a book in the [genre] category. Please generate a list of creative book ideas, including a brief synopsis, potential themes, and a unique hook that makes each story compelling."

5. Marketing Campaign Ideas

"I need creative marketing campaign ideas for my business, which sells [product/service]. The ideas should be innovative, engaging, and suited for digital platforms like social media, email marketing, or influencer partnerships."

6. Event Planning and Theme Ideas

"I am organizing an event for [occasion—birthday, wedding, corporate event, etc.]. Please provide a list of unique theme ideas, decorations, and entertainment suggestions to make it special."

7. Gift Ideas for a Special Occasion

"I need to find the perfect gift for [recipient] for [occasion—birthday, anniversary, holiday, etc.]. Please generate a list of thoughtful, unique, and personalized gift ideas based on their interests."

8. Creative Ways to Make Money Online

"I am looking for ways to earn money online using my skills

in [list skills]. Please generate a list of creative and realistic income-generating ideas, such as freelancing, content creation, or e-commerce."

9. **Engaging Icebreaker Questions or Conversation Starters**

"I want to come up with fun and engaging icebreaker questions for [situation—networking event, team meeting, social gathering, etc.]. Please generate a list of creative questions that spark interesting conversations."

10. **New Hobby or Skill to Learn**

"I want to pick up a new hobby or skill that suits my interests in [area—music, fitness, art, technology, etc.]. Please suggest unique and fulfilling hobbies along with resources or ways to get started."

Personal Assistance

1. **Daily To-Do List Planning**

"I want to create a structured to-do list for my day. My main priorities are [list tasks]. Please organize them into a well-balanced plan, including estimated timeframes and productivity tips."

2. **Meal Planning and Recipe Suggestions**

"I need a weekly meal plan based on my dietary preferences [e.g., vegetarian, high-protein, low-carb] and my available ingredients: [list ingredients]. Please provide meal ideas along with easy-to-follow recipes."

3. Time Management Strategy

"I struggle with managing my time effectively, especially when balancing [work, studies, personal life]. Please suggest a structured time management plan, including productivity techniques and daily routines to stay on track."

4. Travel Itinerary for a Trip

"I am planning a trip to [destination] for [number] days. I'd like an itinerary that includes must-see attractions, local dining recommendations, and efficient travel routes. Please tailor it to a [relaxing/adventurous/cultural] travel style."

5. Exercise and Fitness Plan

"I want to create a fitness plan that helps me achieve [goal—weight loss, muscle gain, endurance]. My current fitness level is [beginner/intermediate/advanced], and I prefer [home workouts, gym sessions, outdoor activities]. Please provide a weekly workout schedule."

6. Personal Budget Planning

"I need help setting up a personal budget to manage my income of [$X] per month. My expenses include [list main expenses]. Please create a structured budget that helps me save money while covering essential costs."

7. Decluttering and Organization Plan

"I want to declutter and organize my [home, office, digital files]. Please provide a step-by-step plan that helps me efficiently sort, clean, and maintain an organized space."

8. Self-Care Routine Recommendations

"I need a self-care routine that helps me manage stress and

improve my well-being. My schedule is [busy/flexible], and I prefer activities like [list preferred self-care practices]. Please create a personalized self-care plan."

9. Guided Reflection for Personal Growth

"I want to reflect on my personal growth over the past year. Please provide thought-provoking journal prompts that help me assess my achievements, challenges, and goals for the future."

10. Gift-Wrapping and Presentation Ideas

"I am giving a gift to [recipient] for [occasion], and I want the presentation to be unique and memorable. Please suggest creative gift-wrapping ideas and personal touches that will make it special."

Social Interaction

1. Starting a Conversation with a New Acquaintance

"I'm meeting someone new in a [social/professional] setting, and I want to start a natural and engaging conversation. Please provide a few conversation starters and follow-up questions that help build rapport."

2. Apologizing and Repairing a Relationship

"I need to apologize to [person] for [situation]. The apology should be sincere, acknowledge my mistake, and express my willingness to make amends. Please write a message that conveys my sincerity while maintaining a positive tone."

3. Expressing Gratitude in a Meaningful Way

"I want to send a heartfelt message to [friend, family member, coworker] expressing my gratitude for [reason]. Please craft a warm and genuine thank-you note that highlights my appreciation."

4. Navigating a Difficult Conversation

"I need to have a difficult conversation with [person] about [topic]. The message should be respectful, clear, and empathetic while addressing my concerns. Please help me phrase it in a way that encourages open communication."

5. Reaching Out to an Old Friend

"I haven't spoken to [friend's name] in a long time, and I want to reconnect. Please draft a friendly message that feels natural and warm, without making it awkward."

6. Inviting Someone to an Event

"I'm inviting [person or group] to [event—party, dinner, networking event]. The invitation should be warm, clear, and include all necessary details while encouraging them to attend. Please craft a compelling message."

7. Responding to a Compliment or Praise

"Someone has given me a compliment or positive feedback about [specific achievement or quality]. I want to respond in a way that is appreciative and confident without sounding dismissive. Please provide a well-balanced response."

8. Encouraging Someone Who Is Struggling

"A friend or family member is going through a tough time with [situation]. I want to send an encouraging and supportive message that lifts their spirits and shows I care. Please write

something empathetic and uplifting."

9. Expressing Interest in a Romantic Way

"I like [person's name] and want to express my interest in a way that is charming, respectful, and not too forward. Please provide a message or conversation approach that feels natural and engaging."

10. Defusing a Tense or Awkward Situation

"I found myself in an awkward or tense moment with [person] regarding [situation]. I need a way to ease the tension and bring the conversation back to a positive or neutral place. Please suggest a message or approach to handle it smoothly."

Chapter Ten

AI at Work: Boosting Productivity

P icture this: You're in an office, surrounded by a mountain of paperwork, your phone ringing off the hook, and an email inbox that seems to multiply like rabbits. Now, imagine a magical helper who can sort, manage, and even predict what you need before you start pulling your hair out. This is not a fairy tale. This is the world of AI at work, where productivity gets a turbo boost, leaving you with more time to do the things that truly matter—like finally taking that lunch break away from your desk. In this chapter, we explore how AI can transform your business operations, turning chaos into calm and making you wonder how you ever survived without it.

AI for Business: Streamlining Operations

In the bustling world of business, where time is money and every second counts, AI steps in like a superhero, ready to save the day. One of the most impressive feats AI can perform is automating routine business processes. Imagine AI tools swooping in to handle those pesky repetitive tasks that consume your day, leaving you free to focus on more strategic activities. Take invoice processing, for example. Instead of spending hours manually entering data into spreadsheets, AI can automate this task with the precision of a laser-guided missile. It captures and organizes information with minimal human intervention, ensuring accuracy and saving you from the tedium of endless data entry.

Order management is another area where AI flexes its muscles. By automating the entire process, from order placement to fulfillment, AI ensures that everything runs smoothly, without the usual hiccups. It tracks orders, monitors inventory levels, and even predicts potential issues before they arise. It's like having a crystal ball for your business, allowing you to make informed decisions and keep your customers happy. Speaking of customers, AI-powered chatbots are revolutionizing customer service. These digital assistants handle inquiries with ease, providing instant responses and solving problems faster than you can say "Let me check on that for you." They're available 24/7, ensuring that your customers always have access to the support they need, without the wait.

AI doesn't just handle the grunt work; it also enhances decision-making by providing valuable insights. Predictive analytics is a game-changer for inventory management, analyzing historical data to forecast demand and optimize stock levels. It's like having a weather forecast for your inventory, ensuring you never run out of umbrellas during a rainstorm. AI-driven market trend analysis offers a glimpse into the future, identifying emerging patterns and helping you stay ahead of the competition. By leveraging these insights, businesses can make smarter decisions, reduce waste, and maximize profits.

The supply chain is the backbone of many businesses, and AI is transforming it into a well-oiled machine. Demand forecasting with AI enhances efficiency by predicting customer needs and adjusting production schedules accordingly. This not only reduces waste but also ensures that products are available when customers want them. Route optimization for logistics takes the guesswork out of delivery planning, minimizing travel time and fuel consumption. It's like having a GPS that knows the fastest, most efficient route before you even start the engine. With AI, the supply chain becomes a seamless operation, boosting productivity and reducing costs.

Customer relationships are the lifeblood of any business, and AI technologies are redefining how we engage with and retain them. AI-powered customer relationship management (CRM) systems provide a comprehensive view of customer interactions, enabling personalized marketing strategies that resonate with individual preferences. It's like having a personal shopper for each customer, ensuring they feel valued and understood. By leveraging AI insights, businesses can create tailored experiences that foster loyalty and drive growth. So, whether you're a small business owner or part of a large corporation, AI offers solutions that streamline operations, enhance decision-making, and improve customer engagement, leaving you with more time to focus on what you do best.

Smart Communication: AI in Emails and Correspondence

Imagine a world where your email inbox doesn't feel like a never-ending avalanche of messages threatening to bury you alive. AI tools have come to the rescue, transforming the way we handle emails and correspondence. These digital assistants are like the magical elves of the email world, quietly working behind the scenes to ensure everything runs smoothly. Automated email responses are a game-changer, handling routine queries and responses with the efficiency of a seasoned diplomat. They sort and categorize emails faster than you can say "inbox zero," ensuring that important messages never slip through the cracks. With AI, you can set up automated follow-ups and reminders, making sure you never forget to respond to that crucial client email or Aunt Martha's invitation to Sunday brunch. These tools free up your time, allowing you to focus on the emails that truly matter, while ensuring that nothing important gets left behind.

Drafting emails can often feel like trying to write a novel with only half the alphabet, but AI is here to make that task a breeze. AI's role in crafting and fine-tuning emails ensures that every message you send is clear, concise, and professional. With AI-generated email templates, you never have to start from scratch. These templates provide a solid foundation, allowing you to tailor each message to suit its recipient. It's like having a skeleton key that fits every lock, ensuring your emails are always on point. But it doesn't stop there. Grammar and tone-checking tools polish your prose to perfection, catching those pesky typos and ensuring your tone matches the content. Whether you're negotiating a business deal or sending a quick thank-you note, AI ensures your emails are as polished as a pair of shiny new shoes.

Managing an overflowing inbox can feel like trying to herd cats, but AI is the shepherd you didn't know you needed. These tools help you organize and prioritize emails with the finesse of a master conductor. Smart inbox filtering means you can sort messages by importance, sender, or even subject matter, making it easier to find what you need when you need it. Priority email highlighting ensures that crucial messages rise to the top, catching your attention before they get lost in the shuffle. It's like having a personal assistant who knows exactly what you need to see first, and who never misplaces a memo. By streamlining email management, AI allows you to take control of your inbox, reducing stress and increasing productivity.

In today's globalized world, language barriers are a thing of the past, thanks to AI translation tools. Seamless multilingual communication is within reach, whether you're negotiating with a business partner in Tokyo or planning a family reunion in Paris. Real-time email translation services make it easy to communicate across languages, ensuring your message is understood no matter who receives it. It's like having a Babel fish in your ear, translating as you type. Multilingual chatbot integrations further enhance communication, allowing businesses to provide customer support in multiple languages simultaneously. Whether you're reaching out to a colleague overseas or assisting a customer in another country, AI ensures that language is no longer a barrier but a bridge.

Data Simplified: AI for Reports and Analysis

Imagine a world where data entry doesn't involve hours of squinting at spreadsheets or deciphering handwritten notes that look like a doctor's prescription. Welcome to the era of AI, where Optical Character Recognition (OCR) technology is your new best friend. This nifty tool can scan documents faster than you can say "data overload" and accurately convert printed text into digital data. Whether it's invoices, receipts, or any other type of paperwork, OCR saves you from a mountain of manual labor while reducing the risk of those inevitable human errors sneaking in. It's like having a personal assistant with eyes sharper than an eagle, capable of processing information in record time.

But what about extracting data from those endless documents that seem to multiply overnight? AI's got you covered there, too. Automated data extraction tools sift through files, pulling out relevant information with the precision of a master chef separating egg yolks from whites. These tools can identify key data points from a sea of text, ensuring that nothing gets missed. This not only speeds up the process but also ensures that the extracted data is ready for analysis, letting you focus on the insights rather than the input. It's a bit like having a librarian who can find that obscure book in the back of the library without breaking a sweat.

Once AI has worked its magic on data entry, it's time to transform that raw data into something meaningful. This is where AI-driven data visualization comes into play. Imagine complex datasets turning into easy-to-understand graphs and charts, like watching a chaotic orchestra suddenly playing in perfect harmony. These visualizations are more than just pretty pictures; they provide a clear, concise view of trends and patterns that might otherwise go unnoticed. It's as if AI hands you a pair of glasses that bring your data into sharp focus, making it easier to make informed decisions. And when it comes to understanding customer feedback, sentiment analysis tools decode the nuances of customer opinions, translating abstract sentiments into actionable insights. These tools can tell you if your latest product launch was the talk of the town or just a whisper in the wind, allowing you to adjust your strategies accordingly.

AI doesn't stop at analyzing data; it also excels in enhancing the accuracy and speed of reporting. Real-time report generation tools are like having a news ticker for your business, constantly updating you with the latest insights and metrics. Gone are the days of waiting for reports to be compiled and double-checked. AI automates this process, producing detailed reports that you can trust in a fraction of the time. Automated financial reporting takes the stress out of quarterly reviews, ensuring that your financial data is not only accurate but also ready when you need it. It's like having an accountant who never takes a coffee break or files your taxes late.

Predictive analytics is where AI truly shines, with the ability to forecast trends and outcomes with astonishing accuracy. Imagine having a crystal ball that doesn't just show you the present but predicts the future with data-driven precision. AI-powered sales trend predictions can help you anticipate demand, ensuring you have the right products at the right time. Meanwhile, customer behavior forecasting models give you insights into what your customers might want next, allowing you to tailor your offerings to meet their needs. It's like having a sixth sense for business, giving you an edge over competitors who are still relying on yesterday's data to make today's decisions. With AI, you're not just keeping up; you're setting the pace in a rapidly changing world.

Virtual Meetings: AI-Assisted Agendas and Notes

Ever felt like meetings are the black holes of productivity, sucking up time and energy without mercy? Fear not, for AI is here to rescue you from the abyss of endless meetings with its array of virtual superpowers. Imagine AI as your personal meeting planner, one that not only keeps track of time but also creates and distributes agendas with the precision of a Swiss watchmaker. AI-generated agenda suggestions mean you no longer have to rack your brain trying to remember what needs to be discussed. It's like having a mind reader who knows exactly what's important and what's just fluff. Once the agenda is set, automated distribution ensures everyone involved is on the same page before the meeting even begins, reducing the risk of those awkward moments where everyone stares blankly at each other, wondering who's supposed to speak first.

Now, let's talk about note-taking, a task that often feels like trying to catch a hurricane in a teacup. AI tools equipped with real-time transcription services swoop in to save the day, capturing every word with the accuracy of a seasoned court reporter. Forget about scribbling frantically and missing half the conversation; AI captures it all, allowing you to focus on participating instead of writing. After the meeting, summarization tools do the heavy lifting, distilling key discussion points into concise, digestible summaries. It's like having a personal editor who turns a novel's worth of notes into a neatly organized short story. No more deciphering cryptic shorthand or trying to remember who said what—AI keeps it all straight for you.

Once the meeting wraps up, it's easy to feel overwhelmed by the tidal wave of action items and follow-up tasks. But AI is here to organize your chaos like a seasoned librarian sorting through a mountain of returned books. Automated task assignment ensures each item is allocated to the right person, with the precision of a chess master making the perfect move. Reminder systems kick in, gently nudging you and your team to keep things on track without the need for nagging emails or missed deadlines. It's like having a personal assistant who never forgets and always knows when to prod you into action.

Participation and engagement are the keys to successful meetings, but let's face it, sometimes it's hard to keep everyone focused. AI enhances virtual meeting experiences by analyzing engagement metrics, ensuring every participant stays involved and contributes. This isn't Big Brother watching; it's more like a helpful coach guiding everyone to the finish line. Virtual backgrounds and noise cancellation features keep distractions at bay, turning your cluttered kitchen or noisy coffee shop into a professional meeting space with the click of a button. Imagine the pleasure of a meeting where the only sounds you hear are relevant discussions, not the neighbor's dog barking or the barista's espresso machine hissing in the background.

Finally, AI ensures that virtual meetings are not just a necessary evil but a productive and enjoyable part of your work life. By streamlining preparation, enhancing note-taking, facilitating follow-ups, and improving engagement, AI transforms meetings from a mundane task into an efficient, almost pleasant experience. Whether you're managing a team from a bustling office or coordinating with colleagues from the comfort of your living room, AI ensures that your virtual meetings run as smoothly as a well-oiled machine.

Collaborative Tools: Enhancing Teamwork with AI

Imagine a world where working with your team feels as seamless as a well-rehearsed dance, regardless of where everyone is located. AI has transformed collaboration into an effortless symphony, harmonizing teamwork across different locations and time zones. Picture platforms like Slack, now supercharged with AI enhancements, enabling instant communication that feels as natural as chatting with a colleague over coffee. These platforms are your digital watercoolers, where ideas flow freely across continents with just a keystroke. Real-time document collaboration tools further break down barriers, allowing multiple people to work simultaneously on the same file without stepping on each other's toes. It's like having a whiteboard that everyone can reach, even if they're miles apart.

Project management has always been a bit like herding cats, but AI is here to bring some order to the chaos. AI-driven project management software acts as the conductor of your team's symphony, ensuring that every task gets the attention it deserves. By analyzing workloads and deadlines, AI helps prioritize tasks and allocate resources efficiently. It's like having a personal project manager who never takes a day off and always knows which task is the star of the show. This technology doesn't just keep track of what needs to be done; it optimizes the entire process, ensuring your team hits all the right notes. Project management software isn't just a tool; it's a partner in productivity, ensuring every project is a success.

Communication within a team can sometimes feel like trying to speak through a tin can and string, but AI is here to upgrade your connection. Sentiment analysis tools act like an emotional barometer, gauging the mood of your team and providing insights into team dynamics. It's like having a therapist on call, ensuring everyone is heard and understood. AI chatbots for internal support offer quick answers and information, acting as the go-to resource for any questions your team might have. Whether it's clarifying a process or finding a document, these bots ensure that no question goes unanswered. It's like having an encyclopedia that talks back, providing support and keeping the team moving forward.

Innovation and creativity are often sparked in the most unexpected places, and AI is the catalyst that encourages these eureka moments. AI brainstorming tools are like a never-ending idea factory, churning out concepts and solutions that push the boundaries of conventional thinking. Imagine using AI to facilitate idea generation, with platforms that suggest new angles and perspectives you might not have considered. It's like having an endless supply of sticky notes, each one with a fresh idea waiting to be explored. These tools don't just inspire creativity; they nurture it, creating an environment where every team member feels empowered to contribute.

In the grand scheme of things, AI isn't just a tool; it's a collaborator that enhances teamwork and fosters innovation. It breaks down barriers, creating a workspace where creativity and productivity thrive. By integrating AI, teams can work more effectively and efficiently, turning challenges into opportunities for growth and success. As we wrap up our discussion on AI in the workplace, it's clear that these tools are more than just technological advancements—they're the future of how we work together. Now, with AI as your ally, you're ready to tackle any project with confidence and creativity, transforming the ordinary into the extraordinary.

Chapter Eleven

Ethical and Social Implications of AI

Picture yourself at a dinner party, where the main dish is a technological curiosity, and the guests are intrigued but a tad anxious about the mysterious AI hors d'oeuvres. While everyone's eager to dig in, there's a murmur of concern about what's ethically on the menu. Welcome to the world of AI ethics—a topic that's as essential as remembering to season your soup. In a world increasingly driven by algorithms and code, understanding AI ethics is like having a GPS for navigating this digital landscape. Without it, we risk getting lost in a maze of moral dilemmas and not-so-pleasant surprises. So, what exactly are AI ethics? Think of them as the guiding principles that ensure AI behaves more like a helpful neighbor and less like a rogue software that's out to steal your Wi-Fi. These principles emphasize transparency and accountability, two crucial elements that ensure AI systems are not only effective but also trustworthy.

Transparency in AI is akin to reading the ingredients on your favorite cereal box. It's about knowing what's inside and how it affects you. When AI systems are transparent, users can understand how decisions are made, ensuring there are no hidden surprises. Accountability, on the other hand, is like having a responsible babysitter for your digital life, ensuring that AI systems function as intended and that there's someone to answer when things go awry. The UNESCO Recommendation on AI Ethics underscores these principles, advocating for human oversight and emphasizing the importance of protecting human rights and dignity. This is not just a lofty ideal; it's a practical necessity for maintaining trust and ensuring AI serves humanity's best interests.

However, achieving ethical AI is not without its challenges—chief among them being bias. Imagine AI as a chef with a penchant for spicy food, serving dishes that leave some diners reaching for water. Bias in AI systems can lead to unfair outcomes, where certain groups are favored over others, much like a restaurant that only serves one type of cuisine. This bias often stems from historical data, which can reflect societal prejudices. Take, for example, the case of the COMPAS software, which was found to exhibit racial bias in predicting recidivism. Such biases highlight the need for careful consideration in algorithm design, ensuring that AI decisions are fair and unbiased. By addressing these issues, we can prevent AI from becoming a digital echo chamber that amplifies existing inequalities.

To promote fairness and inclusivity, we must ensure that AI systems are designed to treat all users equitably. Techniques for bias mitigation are crucial in this endeavor. Pre-processing methods, like relabelling and perturbation, help cleanse datasets before they even reach AI models, much like washing vegetables before cooking. In-processing methods adjust algorithms during training, ensuring they don't develop a taste for discrimination. Post-processing methods ensure that the final AI output is as balanced as a perfectly seasoned dish.

These strategies are essential for creating AI systems that serve everyone equally, without leaving a bitter aftertaste. Ensuring diverse training datasets is also vital, as it broadens AI's perspective and helps it better understand the complexities of the world.

Encouraging ethical AI practices requires industry-wide commitment and adherence to guidelines that promote responsible development and deployment. Much like following a recipe to create a culinary masterpiece, developers must adhere to ethical guidelines that emphasize fairness, privacy, and accountability. These guidelines act as a moral compass, guiding developers in creating systems that respect user rights and prioritize societal welfare. Moreover, fostering a culture of ethical awareness within the AI community is crucial. By encouraging discussions and collaboration, we can establish industry-wide standards that ensure AI systems are developed with the highest ethical considerations. This collective effort will help prevent AI from becoming a runaway train, ensuring it remains a tool for positive change and progress.

Interactive Element: Reflect on AI Ethics

Consider a recent AI interaction you've experienced, whether it was a recommendation from a streaming service or an automated customer service chat. Ask yourself: Was the interaction transparent? Did it feel fair? Reflect on these questions and jot down your thoughts. This exercise helps cultivate an awareness of AI ethics in everyday experiences, empowering you to engage with technology more thoughtfully. By recognizing the ethical dimensions of AI, you become an informed user, capable of advocating for systems that align with our shared values of fairness, transparency, and accountability.

Privacy and Security: Protecting Your Data with AI

Imagine AI as both the hero and the villain in the grand opera of data privacy. On one hand, it offers cutting-edge encryption technologies that protect your personal information like a digital fortress. It's the digital equivalent of a super-sleuth, using complex algorithms to encrypt your data, ensuring that even the most seasoned hackers are left scratching their heads. This AI-driven encryption acts as a shield, transforming your data into a jigsaw puzzle that only the right key can solve. But, not all is rosy in the land of digital defense. AI also presents risks, especially when it comes to data breaches. In its pursuit of efficiency, AI can inadvertently become a double agent, exposing vulnerabilities that cybercriminals are all too eager to exploit. These breaches can lead to unauthorized access, where your data is handled as carelessly as a toddler with a bowl of spaghetti. Striking the right balance between protection and vulnerability is a dance that requires vigilance and innovation.

Enter AI's role as a cybersecurity sentinel, a watchful guardian standing at the gates of your digital life. AI applications in cybersecurity are akin to having a digital watchdog that never sleeps. They utilize sophisticated algorithms for threat detection, scanning for anomalies that could indicate a potential attack. It's like having a security system that not only tells you when the door is ajar but also predicts when intruders might strike. Real-time intrusion prevention systems take it a step further, acting swiftly to neutralize threats before they can wreak havoc. These systems are the unsung heroes of data integrity, ensuring your information remains as intact as a perfectly baked soufflé. By analyzing patterns and making decisions faster than a caffeine-fueled night owl, AI enhances cybersecurity measures, keeping your data safe from the lurking shadows of the netherworld.

Yet, with great power comes great responsibility, and AI's capabilities in surveillance raise significant ethical concerns. Consider facial recognition technology, a tool that recognizes faces faster than you can say "cheese." While it offers convenience, such as unlocking your phone with a glance, it also poses a threat to privacy. Imagine a world where every public space is a potential surveillance hotspot, where your every move is tracked with the precision of a hawk. The societal impact of AI-powered surveillance is profound, blurring the lines between security and intrusion. Balancing these two is like walking a tightrope, where one misstep could lead to a loss of privacy or, conversely, a security breach. It's a delicate act that requires constant evaluation and thoughtful regulation to ensure that AI serves the public good without infringing on individual rights.

In this AI-driven world, responsible data management is not just a good idea; it's a necessity. Best practices for managing personal data responsibly are akin to having a roadmap for navigating the digital landscape. Data minimization techniques ensure that only the necessary information is collected, much like packing only the essentials for a weekend getaway. Anonymization techniques take it a step further, ensuring that personal identifiers are removed, transforming sensitive data into an unidentifiable soup of numbers and letters. Transparency in data collection practices is crucial, akin to providing a clear menu of what data is being collected and why. Users should know how their data is being used, much like knowing what's in a dish before taking a bite. This openness fosters trust, ensuring that AI systems are not just powerful but also respectful of the individuals they serve.

As we navigate this digital age, it's important to remember that AI is a tool, not a panacea. It's here to assist, not dominate, offering solutions that protect and empower rather than control and exploit. By embracing responsible data management and maintaining a vigilant eye on privacy concerns, we can harness AI's potential for good while safeguarding the rights and freedoms we hold dear. AI's role in privacy and security is a testament to its dual nature, a reminder that while it can be a formidable ally, it requires careful handling to prevent it from becoming a potential adversary.

The Social Impact of AI: A Balanced Perspective

Imagine a world where every scroll through your social media feed feels like it was custom-made for you. In many ways, it is. AI plays a pivotal role in shaping what we see, like a digital curator who knows your preferences better than your best friend. Social media platforms use AI to manage vast amounts of data, determining what posts, ads, and news articles appear on your screen. This personalization can be a double-edged sword. On one hand, it helps users discover content that aligns with their interests, making them feel understood and engaged. On the other hand, it can create echo chambers, where users are only exposed to viewpoints that reinforce their own, potentially deepening divides and polarizing communities. It's like living in a bubble where everyone agrees with you, which sounds great until you need to navigate the real world, where differing opinions abound.

In the realm of education, AI has the potential to be transformative, like a magic wand capable of tailoring learning experiences to individual needs. Personalized learning with AI adapts to each student's pace and style, ensuring that no one is left behind. Picture a classroom where every child receives a customized lesson plan, designed to address their unique strengths and weaknesses. AI tutors offer extra help when needed, providing explanations and practice problems until the student grasps the concept. This individualized attention can boost confidence and foster a love of learning. However, the use of AI in education also raises questions about data privacy and the potential for over-reliance on technology. While AI can provide valuable support, it's important to remember that it should complement, not replace, human interaction and guidance.

When it comes to healthcare, AI is like a doctor with perfect recall, analyzing vast amounts of data to improve patient care. AI diagnostic tools can quickly identify patterns that might elude even the most experienced practitioners, leading to faster and more accurate diagnoses. Imagine a world where illnesses are caught earlier, treatments are more effective, and patient outcomes improve. AI can also help manage patient care by monitoring vital signs and predicting potential health issues before they become critical. However, the integration of AI in healthcare is not without its challenges. Ethical concerns arise around data security and the potential for AI to make decisions without human oversight. It's crucial that AI complements the expertise of healthcare professionals, maintaining the delicate balance between technology and the human touch.

As we navigate this AI-driven world, digital literacy and inclusion become increasingly important. Understanding how to interact with AI technologies is like learning a new language; it opens doors to endless possibilities. Educational initiatives aimed at boosting AI literacy can empower individuals to engage confidently with technology, ensuring they are not left behind in this digital age. Bridging the digital divide is also crucial, as access to AI technologies can significantly impact one's ability to participate in modern society. Equitable access to AI means providing the necessary tools and resources to all, regardless of socioeconomic status. It's about leveling the playing field, ensuring that everyone has the opportunity to benefit from the advancements AI offers.

In this ever-evolving landscape, it's important to recognize the profound social impact AI has on our lives. It influences how we communicate, learn, and receive healthcare, shaping the very fabric of our communities. While AI offers immense potential for positive change, it's essential to approach its integration thoughtfully, considering the ethical implications and striving for inclusivity and fairness. As we continue to explore the possibilities AI presents, we must remain vigilant, ensuring that its development and deployment serve the greater good, fostering a society that is not only technologically advanced but also ethically sound.

AI and Employment: Navigating the Job Landscape

Imagine walking into a workplace where robots and humans work side by side, like a futuristic buddy cop movie. This is not a scene from a sci-fi flick; it's the reality of today's job market, where AI is making waves. The rise of AI automation is reshaping employment, bringing both opportunities and challenges. On one hand, AI can take on mundane tasks, freeing up human workers for more complex duties. Think of it like having a diligent assistant who never clocks out. However, with this comes the fear of job displacement, as machines learn to do more. Automation might lead to certain roles becoming obsolete, much like how email replaced the fax machine. But before you panic and start stockpiling canned goods, know that AI is also creating new roles. The tech industry, for instance, is booming with positions that didn't exist a decade ago. From data scientists to AI ethicists, these new jobs require skills that are as fresh as this morning's coffee.

With these changes come the inevitable need for reskilling and upskilling. It's like getting a software update for your career, ensuring you're equipped with the latest features. Traditional skills might not cut it in an AI-driven world, much like trying to play a Blu-ray disc in a VHS player. Thankfully, there are training programs designed to bridge this gap, offering courses in AI-related skills. These programs are popping up faster than pop-up ads, provided by both government initiatives and private sector efforts. They focus on equipping workers with the knowledge needed to thrive in an AI-dominated job market. It's like going back to school, but without the cafeteria food. This adaptation is crucial, ensuring that workers are not left behind as industries evolve. By embracing these educational opportunities, you can transform your career from a horse-and-buggy operation to a sleek, high-speed train.

But don't just focus on the potential downsides. AI is also a catalyst for job creation, opening doors to industries ripe with innovation. It's like planting seeds that grow into fields of opportunity. In creative industries, AI acts as a co-creator, helping artists, writers, and musicians push boundaries. Imagine composing music with an AI partner, where every note is a surprise, or designing fashion with AI that predicts the next trend before it hits the runway. AI roles in data analysis and management are also on the rise, as organizations seek to harness the power of data. These roles are as crucial as the air traffic controllers of the digital world, guiding companies through the complex skies of information. As AI continues to expand, new industries will emerge, offering opportunities for those willing to explore uncharted territories.

Ethical workforce transition is key to navigating this new landscape. It's about ensuring that as we move forward, no one is left behind. Supporting displaced workers with retraining programs is crucial, helping them find new paths in the evolving job market. It's like offering a lifeline to those adrift in a sea of change. These programs provide the skills needed to transition into new roles, ensuring workers can continue to thrive. Fair treatment in AI-driven work environments is also vital, ensuring that employees are respected and valued, regardless of the technological changes around them. This is about creating workplaces where humans and AI coexist harmoniously, like a well-rehearsed orchestra playing in perfect harmony.

In this new era, the job market is both a challenge and an opportunity. AI is reshaping the landscape, requiring adaptation and innovation. By focusing on reskilling, embracing new opportunities, and ensuring ethical transitions, we can navigate this terrain successfully. The future of work is not a dystopian nightmare but a chance to reimagine what's possible. As we move forward, let's do so with curiosity and optimism, ready to embrace the changes that AI brings.

As we transition from exploring employment to understanding AI's broader implications, we turn our gaze towards the future. The next chapter will delve into how AI continues to shape our daily lives, offering insights and innovations that redefine what it means to live in a technologically advanced society. Join me as we explore the transformative potential of AI beyond the workplace.

Chapter Twelve

AI for Personal Growth and Learning

Picture this: You, lounging in your favorite chair, sipping a cup of tea, while AI acts as your personal tutor, transforming your living room into a classroom of endless possibilities. Sounds delightful, doesn't it? In today's digital age, the classroom is no longer confined to brick and mortar. With AI-driven educational platforms like Coursera and Khan Academy, you have access to a treasure trove of knowledge at your fingertips, tailored just for you. These platforms are like having a dedicated tutor who knows your strengths, weaknesses, and when you need a nudge to keep going. Whether you're brushing up on algebra or diving into the intricacies of art history, AI ensures that your learning path is as unique as your fingerprint, mapping out a course that's designed to fit your personal learning style and pace.

One of the marvels of AI in education is its ability to adapt and personalize learning experiences to suit individual needs. Imagine a classroom where lessons adjust in real-time to match your learning speed, offering feedback the moment you need it. This is not a far-fetched science fiction plot but a reality made possible by AI. It's like having a tutor who's not only patient but also incredibly perceptive, able to tweak difficulty levels on the fly, ensuring you're always challenged but never overwhelmed. This adaptive learning approach transforms traditional education into a dynamic, learner-centered experience, where the lessons you engage with are as flexible as a yoga instructor with a penchant for problem-solving.

Interactive simulations powered by AI offer an immersive way to dive into complex subjects, making learning not just educational but also engaging. Picture yourself donning a virtual lab coat, conducting experiments in a digital laboratory where safety goggles are optional, and mistakes are merely stepping stones to understanding. These virtual labs allow you to experiment with different variables without the risk of explosions or costly mishaps. It's like playing with a chemistry set that's smarter than your average bear. Historical event reconstructions place you smack dab in the middle of pivotal moments in time, allowing you to explore history as if you had your own personal time machine, minus the risk of altering the space-time continuum.

The beauty of AI-driven learning is that it puts you in the driver's seat, allowing you to set the pace and direction of your educational journey. With flexible scheduling and AI reminders, you can learn at your own speed without guilt or pressure. Whether you're a night owl who thrives in the moonlight or an early bird who likes to seize the day, AI accommodates your schedule, ensuring that education fits seamlessly into your life. Progress tracking and milestone achievements act as your personal cheerleaders, celebrating your victories and nudging you gently if you start to wander off the path. It's like having a supportive friend who always knows when to high-five you and when to offer a gentle push in the right direction.

Interactive Element: Find Your Learning Path

As you embark on this educational adventure with AI, consider exploring platforms like Coursera or Khan Academy. Browse their courses and see which subjects pique your interest. Use their AI-driven tools to assess your current knowledge level and set achievable learning goals. Take note of the personalized learning paths and recommendations offered, and reflect on how they align with your interests and aspirations. Keep a journal of your progress, noting milestones achieved and new insights gained. This reflection exercise will help you stay focused and motivated as you navigate your personal learning journey.

Language Learning with AI: A New Approach

Imagine cracking open the secrets of a new language with the ease of tapping an app on your phone. AI-powered language learning apps like Duolingo and Babbel have turned this fantasy into reality. They're like having a patient language tutor who never gets tired of your mispronunciations. Duolingo, with its gamified lessons, transforms learning into a daily habit that feels more like playing a game than studying. Babbel offers a structured curriculum that immerses you in real-world conversations, making the leap from textbook language to everyday use. These apps integrate AI to enhance your pronunciation through speech recognition technology, offering feedback that rivals a native speaker's ear. It's like having a pocket-sized language coach who always has time for a quick practice session, whether you're waiting for your coffee or on your commute to work.

As you engage with these apps, you'll find that AI tools offer more than just vocabulary lists and grammar rules. They're interactive companions that adapt to your learning style, providing real-time corrections that help polish your language skills. Imagine having a conversation simulation where AI serves as both your conversation partner and instructor, gently nudging you toward correct usage and helping you avoid those embarrassing faux pas. It's the perfect setup for gaining confidence in your language abilities without the pressure of performing in front of a live audience. AI provides the feedback loop you need to refine your skills, ensuring that your "bonjour" sounds less like "bone-jour" and more like a warm Parisian greeting.

But language is more than words; it's culture, context, and nuance. AI steps in here as well, providing cultural immersion experiences that elevate your learning from rote memorization to genuine understanding. Imagine AI-generated scenarios where you navigate a bustling market in Marrakesh or sip espresso at a café in Rome, engaging in dialogues that deepen your comprehension of cultural subtleties. These scenarios are like virtual field trips that bring the language to life, allowing you to practice contextual language use without booking a flight. Virtual reality environments further enhance this experience, immersing you in the sights and sounds of your target language's culture, making the learning process as enriching as it is educational.

AI also plays a vital role in breaking down language barriers and fostering multilingual interactions. Real-time translation apps, such as Google Translate, are like having a personal interpreter in your pocket, ready to assist whenever words fail you. Whether you're deciphering a menu in Tokyo or negotiating a business deal in Berlin, AI-driven translation ensures you're never at a loss for words. Language exchange platforms powered by AI offer opportunities to practice with native speakers, bridging the gap between learners and fluent speakers. These platforms provide a dynamic space for cultural exchange, where you can practice your skills, learn from others, and maybe even make a friend or two. AI facilitates these connections, making the world feel a little smaller and a lot more connected.

AI in Personal Development: Setting and Achieving Goals

Picture this: you've got aspirations as big as a mountain, but every time you try to climb, you find yourself slipping on the rocks of procrastination and confusion. Enter AI planners, your trusty guides on the path to personal growth. These digital wizards are designed to help you set, organize, and achieve your goals with the precision of a Swiss watch. Imagine having an app that not only keeps track of your ambitions but also nudges you with suggestions based on the SMART goal framework—specific, measurable, achievable, relevant, and time-bound. It's like having a wise old mentor in your pocket, whispering the secrets of success.

With AI-driven goal-setting apps, you can break down your lofty ambitions into manageable steps. These apps are a bit like having a personal coach who knows exactly when to push you harder and when to let you coast. They help you define clear objectives, set deadlines, and even suggest strategies to overcome obstacles. Need to run a marathon or finally tackle that novel you've been dreaming about? These apps create a roadmap that leads you from start to finish, ensuring you're not just dreaming but doing. The beauty is in the data, providing insights that help you understand your progress and adjust your path if needed. Each goal becomes a project, complete with timelines and milestones, transforming your ambitions into tangible achievements.

But setting goals is only half the battle. Staying motivated and tracking progress is where the magic happens. AI-powered dashboards offer a visual feast of your accomplishments, painting a picture of your journey with graphs and charts as colorful as a sunrise. These dashboards are like your personal cheer squad, celebrating your victories and encouraging you to push through the tough spots. And just when you feel your motivation waning, AI steps in with motivational prompts and reminders. It's like having a pep talk from your most supportive friend, keeping your spirits high and your feet moving. Whether it's a gentle nudge to get back on track or an inspiring quote to brighten your day, these AI-generated messages ensure you're never alone on your path to personal growth.

Habits, those pesky little critters that can either be your best allies or your worst enemies, are crucial in achieving personal development goals. AI is here to help you form and maintain positive habits with the precision of a habit-tracking guru. These applications provide insights into your daily routines, identifying patterns that may be holding you back and suggesting ways to improve. Imagine receiving a gentle reminder to drink water, stretch, or take a moment to breathe. These AI reminders act like a kind-hearted drill sergeant, ensuring you stick to your routines without becoming overbearing. By reinforcing positive habits, AI helps you build a foundation for long-term success and personal well-being.

Personal development is not a one-size-fits-all endeavor, and AI understands that. It offers personalized self-improvement plans tailored to your unique needs and preferences. Through AI assessments, you gain self-awareness, identifying strengths and areas for growth with the clarity of a mirror. These assessments help you craft customized paths that align with your aspirations and lifestyle. Imagine a plan that not only guides you towards your goals but also adapts as you evolve. It's like having a tailor who adjusts your suit as you change, ensuring the perfect fit every time. AI becomes your partner in growth, supporting you with insights and strategies that propel you forward.

Enhancing Memory and Cognition with AI Tools

Picture this: your brain, a bustling metropolis of neurons, each one like a little worker bee buzzing around, trying to keep everything in order. But let's face it, sometimes the bees get a little tired, and that's where AI steps in with a helping hand. Enter cognitive enhancement apps, designed to whip those neurons into shape and turn your brain into a well-oiled machine. Think of brain training apps like Lumosity as your mental gym, offering a workout without the sweaty gym clothes. These apps employ AI-driven memory exercises and games that are as engaging as they are educational. You can feel your mental muscles flexing as you tackle puzzles and challenges that boost your cognitive functions. It's like having a personal trainer for your brain, except you don't have to worry about skipping leg day.

Memory retention and recall can often feel like trying to grab a slippery fish with your bare hands. Just when you think you've got it, it slips away. AI changes the game with structured exercises that make remembering things a little less like catching fish and more like riding a bike. Spaced repetition algorithms are the secret sauce here, ensuring that information sticks like Velcro. These algorithms are like that friend who reminds you of important dates, repeating them just when you're about to forget. Interactive quizzes offer reinforcement, testing your recall in a way that's both challenging and fun. It's like a pop quiz where the only thing at stake is your pride, and maybe a few bragging rights at the next family gathering.

Cognitive health and wellness might sound like something you'd find in a health magazine, but they're crucial for maintaining your brain's vitality. AI applications are stepping up to the plate, detecting cognitive decline with the precision of a hawk spotting its prey. These tools offer a proactive approach to mental health, flagging potential issues before they become serious. Meanwhile, mental wellness platforms provide AI support that feels like a warm blanket on a cold day. They offer exercises and insights that promote mental agility and flexibility, ensuring your brain stays as sharp as a tack. It's like having a therapist who's available 24/7, offering guidance and support without the hefty price tag.

Now, let's talk about mental agility and flexibility. These are the brain's equivalent of being able to touch your toes without wincing. AI tools encourage this agility through problem-solving games that adjust in complexity as you improve. It's like having a puzzle that grows with you, keeping you on your toes and pushing you to think outside the box. AI-driven creative thinking exercises are like mental yoga, stretching your imagination and encouraging adaptability. They present scenarios that require innovative solutions, prompting you to approach problems from different angles. Imagine facing a challenge and having the mental dexterity to find a solution faster than you can say "Eureka!"

AI's role in enhancing memory and cognition is like having a secret weapon in your quest for mental sharpness. These tools provide the support and structure needed to keep your brain firing on all cylinders, ensuring you're always at the top of your mental game. Whether you're tackling a crossword puzzle, memorizing a speech, or just trying to remember where you left your keys, AI offers the resources to boost your cognitive abilities effortlessly.

Emotional Intelligence: Can AI Help?

Imagine having an insightful friend who helps you understand your emotions better than a therapist with a crystal ball. Enter AI-driven emotional assessment platforms, your digital confidants designed to enhance emotional intelligence and self-awareness. These platforms analyze data from your interactions, offering insights into your emotional patterns that even your best friend might miss. Imagine having a tool that can tell if you're feeling a little blue or on top of the world, offering reasons why and suggesting ways to handle it. It's like having an emotional mirror, reflecting not just your mood but the underlying causes, helping you become more in tune with your feelings than a seasoned yogi.

But what about fostering empathy? AI isn't just about data and numbers; it can simulate human experiences in ways that provoke genuine understanding and compassion. Consider virtual reality empathy exercises, where you can step into someone else's shoes and experience the world from their perspective. Imagine walking a mile in someone else's digital boots, understanding their struggles and triumphs firsthand. AI-generated role-playing scenarios further enhance this experience, allowing you to navigate complex social situations with the finesse of a diplomat. It's akin to rehearsing real-life interactions in a safe, controlled environment, where mistakes are learning opportunities, not social disasters. These simulations cultivate empathy, making you more adept at understanding and connecting with those around you.

Now, let's talk about emotional regulation. Managing emotions can sometimes feel like trying to tame a wild horse, but AI is here to help you hold the reins. AI-guided mindfulness and meditation apps offer a digital sanctuary, where you can retreat whenever stress threatens to overwhelm you. These apps guide you through exercises that calm your mind, helping you find peace amid chaos. Think of them as your personal zen master, whispering words of wisdom and tranquility into your ear. Stress management tools provide insights into your stress patterns, suggesting strategies to keep tension at bay. Imagine having a digital stress-buster, offering techniques tailored to your needs, ensuring you're always ready to face the day's challenges with a cool head.

Interpersonal skills, the social glue that holds relationships together, can be tricky to master. Thankfully, AI is here to lend a hand, or rather, a conversational partner. AI conversation partners are like friendly sparring partners for your social skills, offering a space to practice without fear of judgment. These digital companions provide feedback on both verbal and non-verbal cues, helping you refine your communication finesse. Imagine having a coach who observes your interactions, offering tips to enhance your conversational prowess. It's like having a mirror that reflects not just your words but the subtleties of your body language, ensuring your messages are as clear and impactful as possible.

As we wrap up this exploration of AI in personal growth and learning, it's clear that the digital age offers a plethora of tools to enhance our lives. From emotional intelligence to empathy, AI provides the resources to improve our understanding of ourselves and others. It's not just about technology; it's about using these advancements to become more connected, compassionate, and balanced individuals. Next, we'll shift our focus to the transformative potential of AI in everyday business practices, where efficiency meets innovation in ways that are reshaping industries and careers.

Chapter Thirteen

AI at Work: Boosting Productivity

I magine a world where even your toaster seems to understand the digital age better than your great uncle Ted. While technology sprints ahead like a caffeinated cheetah, many seniors feel like they're left clutching a rotary phone in a 5G world. The common refrain, "I'm too old for this," echoes across generations like a stubborn record that refuses to stop skipping. But what if I told you that AI isn't just for the young techies or the Silicon Valley elite? It's for everyone, including those who remember when phones had cords and televisions had dials. Let's break down those age-related barriers and show you how AI can be as friendly as a neighbor dropping by with a freshly baked pie.

Contrary to popular belief, you don't need a degree in computer science to set up AI devices. Simple guides are your best friend, breaking down the process into easy-to-follow steps that even the most tech-averse can navigate. Imagine setting up a virtual assistant that obeys your every command, without the need to bribe it with cookies. These guides help seniors set up AI devices, whether it's a smart speaker or a health monitoring gadget, ensuring they're connected and confident. Think of it as assembling a jigsaw puzzle, but without that one missing piece that always seems to vanish. And for those who prefer learning in a group, senior-focused workshops and classes provide a supportive environment where questions are encouraged, and no one is left behind. It's like a book club, but instead of discussing the latest thriller, you're uncovering the mysteries of technology.

Once the initial setup is complete, it's time to explore the treasure trove of AI tools designed with seniors in mind. Take health monitoring devices, for example. These gadgets are like having a personal nurse on call 24/7, keeping tabs on vital signs and sending alerts if something seems off. They're not just gadgets; they're lifelines that allow seniors to live independently while ensuring that help is always within reach. Virtual assistants, too, offer more than just weather updates. They remind you to take your medications, keep track of appointments, and even play your favorite tunes on demand. It's like having a personal secretary who never takes a day off and doesn't mind your questionable taste in music.

Let's not forget the social aspect of AI. For seniors who might feel isolated, AI-powered communication apps offer a bridge to family and friends. Imagine video calling your grandkids with the tap of a button, or sending voice messages to your best friend across town. These apps make staying connected as easy as pie, without the need to master the complexities of modern smartphones. And for those looking to expand their social circles, virtual reality experiences open up a world of possibilities. Picture yourself attending a virtual family reunion or joining a book club where members are scattered across the globe. It's not just technology; it's a portal to a wider community.

Real-life stories of seniors embracing AI are as inspiring as they are heartwarming. Take the senior who uses an AI-powered fitness tracker to monitor their daily steps and heart rate. Not only has it motivated them to stay active, but it's also sparked friendly competition with their tech-savvy grandchild. Or consider the grandparent leveraging virtual reality to feel present at family gatherings, even when miles apart. These stories highlight the transformative power of AI, proving that age is just a number when it comes to technology.

Reflection Section: Try It Out!

Consider starting small. If you're new to AI, try setting up a virtual assistant to manage your daily schedule. Explore its features and see how it can simplify your routine. Once you're comfortable, think about expanding into health monitoring or communication apps. Reflect on how these tools enhance your daily life, and share your experiences with friends or family. You might just inspire others to join the digital age with you.

I Don't Have Time: Integrating AI into a Busy Schedule

Life today feels like a never-ending race, with everyone trying to juggle work, family, and the occasional attempt at a social life. If your schedule resembles a chaotic carousel, AI might just be the ticket to slowing things down to a manageable pace. Imagine having an AI-driven personal assistant for task management that doesn't require coffee breaks or sympathy for your Monday blues. These digital marvels can help sort through your daily chaos by organizing tasks, setting priorities, and even reminding you to take that much-needed five-minute meditation break. Automated meal planning apps are a godsend for those evenings when the fridge stares back at you with unspoken judgment.

With AI, you can have meal plans at your fingertips that cater to your dietary needs while optimizing your grocery shopping list, potentially reducing both food waste and trips to the store.

Integrating AI into your daily routine doesn't require a lifestyle overhaul. Start by setting up AI reminders for daily tasks to keep you on track. These smart reminders are more reliable than that sticky note lost to the void of your handbag. They can keep tabs on everything from deadlines at work to watering the plants. For those who find typing on tiny screens a nuisance, speech-to-text AI offers a hands-free note-taking solution that captures your brilliant thoughts as they come, whether you're in the car or cooking dinner. It's like having a personal stenographer who never misses a word, making sure that your next big idea is never forgotten amidst the flurry of daily life.

The benefits of AI extend beyond personal convenience. By enhancing productivity, AI frees up more time for you to engage in personal pursuits. AI tools for quick data analysis can turn hours of number-crunching into minutes, leaving you with more time to focus on strategic thinking rather than spreadsheet staring. Automated scheduling for meetings and appointments removes the hassle of back-and-forth emails, finding common free slots with the finesse of a seasoned diplomat. This means more time for you to engage in activities that truly matter, like spending time with family or pursuing hobbies you never seem to have time for.

The real magic of AI lies in the stories of individuals who have successfully integrated it into their lives. Picture an entrepreneur who uses AI for customer relationship management, allowing them to tailor communications and predict customer needs with uncanny accuracy. This not only enhances client satisfaction but also frees up time that can be invested back into growing the business. Or consider the working parent who employs AI home automation to manage household tasks. From controlling the thermostat to scheduling the robot vac-uum cleaner, AI transforms their home into a place where efficiency reigns, leaving more time for them to enjoy with their children rather than managing chores.

AI is not just a tool—it's a lifestyle enhancer that adapts to our busy lives with ease. It helps us focus on the things that truly matter, ensur-ing that technology serves us, not the other way around. So, whether you're an overworked office dweller, a busy parent, or someone simply trying to carve out a little more 'me' time, AI offers solutions that can make your life feel a bit less like a juggling act and more like a well-choreographed dance. As you explore these new tools, consider how they might fit into your routine, and let them handle the minutiae so you can focus on the big picture.

Does AI Pose a Risk? Addressing Security Concerns

Picture this: you're at a neighborhood barbecue, and someone brings up AI. Suddenly, the conversation shifts to whether robots will one day rule us all. While that might seem like the plot of a sci-fi movie, the real concern isn't about robots taking over but about the security risks that come with AI. Imagine AI systems as vast treasure chests of data. But like any treasure, they need guarding. Data breaches in AI systems are akin to a thief sneaking into your home and rifling through your personal files. These breaches can expose sensitive information, leading to identity theft or financial loss. Meanwhile, AI surveillance technologies raise eyebrows, with questions about privacy and how much of our lives are being watched. It's like having a nosy neighbor peeking over the fence, only the fence is digital and the neighbor is everywhere.

But before you toss your devices out the window, let's talk about keeping those digital fences secure. Best practices for AI security are like gardening tips for a healthy lawn—they keep everything running smoothly. Regular software updates and security patches are crucial. They're like vaccines for your computer, protecting against the latest threats. Strong passwords and authentication measures are your first line of defense, ensuring only you have the keys to your digital kingdom. Think of them as a sturdy lock on your front door, keeping out unwanted guests. These steps might seem basic, but they form the foundation of a robust security strategy.

Privacy concerns with AI are a hot topic, and rightly so. AI can impact privacy in ways we might not immediately notice, like a shadow that's always there but often overlooked. Data encryption techniques play a vital role here. They scramble your information, making it unreadable to anyone without the decryption key. It's like speaking in a secret code only you and your trusted friends understand. Transparency in data usage policies is equally important. You deserve to know how your data is used, like reading the fine print before signing a contract. Companies should be upfront about what they collect and why, ensuring you're informed every step of the way.

To ease any lingering fears, let's hear from the experts. Cybersecurity specialists, who spend their days ensuring our digital safety, offer insights that are both reassuring and practical. One such expert might tell you that the key to managing AI risks is vigilance and preparation. It's about keeping a watchful eye on AI systems, much like how you'd monitor a pot on the stove to prevent boiling over. Case studies of companies implementing secure AI solutions provide a glimpse into how these practices work in real-world scenarios. These businesses demonstrate that with the right measures, AI can be both innovative and secure.

So, while AI is powerful and transformative, like any powerful tool, it needs to be handled with care. Security threats are real but manageable with the right precautions, allowing you to enjoy the benefits of AI without the worry of unwanted surprises.

Practical AI: Beyond the Trend

For anyone who thinks AI is just another tech fad, akin to the pet rock or those dancing hamsters from the early days of the internet, it's time for a reality check. AI is here to stay, and it's playing a starring role in industries that touch every part of our lives. Take healthcare, for instance, where AI isn't just assisting; it's revolutionizing. Imagine algorithms so sharp they can predict patient outcomes or diagnose diseases with accuracy that would make any doctor envious. AI-driven tools are transforming how we approach medical treatment, making it faster, more efficient, and tailored to individual needs. It's like the healthcare equivalent of having a tailor who knows your measurements even better than you do. And don't forget about renewable energy. AI is optimizing wind turbines and solar panels, ensuring they capture every gust of wind and ray of sunshine. This technology isn't just making energy renewable; it's making it smarter, pushing us towards a sustainable future where our energy grids are as intelligent as they are green.

The practical applications of AI extend beyond the individual and into the realm of disaster response and management. When calamity strikes, every second counts, and AI is there to make sure none are wasted. By analyzing data in real-time, AI systems can predict weather patterns or track the spread of wildfires, enabling faster, more precise responses. It's like having a crystal ball that actually works, providing the insights needed to save lives and resources. In agriculture, AI is the unsung hero transforming fields into high-tech hubs of efficiency. From drones that monitor crop health to sensors that optimize irrigation, AI is helping farmers produce more with less. Imagine a world where your salad greens are grown with the assistance of technology that ensures every leaf is as healthy as it can be, and you're beginning to see the impact.

AI's adaptability is what makes it truly remarkable. It evolves, adapts, and meets the ever-changing demands of our world. Take space exploration, where AI is pushing the boundaries of what's possible. From autonomous rovers that explore distant planets to systems that manage the vast amounts of data sent back to Earth, AI is the silent partner in our quest to understand the universe. Personalized medicine is another frontier, where AI analyzes genetic data to develop treatments tailored to individual patients. It's medical care that's as unique as a fingerprint, offering hope for conditions once deemed untreatable. The future of AI isn't just about what it can do today but what it will accomplish tomorrow, as it continuously adapts to our needs.

Forward-thinking AI projects are setting the stage for a future that feels like science fiction brought to life. Autonomous transportation systems are no longer just a concept but a reality, with AI driving innovation in self-driving cars, drones, and even public transport. Cities are becoming smarter, too. Initiatives that use AI to manage traffic flow, reduce energy consumption, and improve public safety are transforming urban landscapes, making them more livable and efficient. Imagine a city where the streetlights adjust based on foot traffic, buses arrive precisely when you need them, and air quality is constantly monitored and improved. AI is the architect of these smart city initiatives, building environments that are not only intelligent but also compassionate, designed to improve quality of life for everyone.

In essence, AI is not a fleeting trend; it's a powerful ally in our pursuit of progress. Its impact is felt across industries, from healthcare and energy to disaster management and agriculture. AI's ability to evolve and adapt ensures that its relevance will only grow, driving innovation and solving problems that once seemed insurmountable. As AI continues to shape our world, it offers a glimpse into a future where technology enhances every aspect of our lives, creating possibilities limited only by our imagination.

Learning from Mistakes: Navigating AI Missteps

In the high-stakes world of AI, mistakes are like papercuts—annoying, sometimes painful, but ultimately a part of learning. One common blunder is over-reliance on AI without human oversight. It's tempting to let AI run the show, especially when it promises efficiency and accuracy. But handing over the reins without a human co-pilot can lead to chaos. AI lacks intuition and empathy, two traits crucial for nuanced decision-making. Imagine a restaurant relying solely on an AI to manage customer service. If a complaint arises about cold soup, the AI might suggest reheating it to boiling point, missing the opportunity for a personal touch like a complimentary dessert. AI should assist, not replace, the human element in customer interactions.

Then there's the issue of inadequate training data, leading to biased outcomes. AI is only as good as the data it consumes. If that data is skewed, the results will follow suit, like feeding a diet of junk food to someone and expecting them to run a marathon. This bias can manifest in various ways, from misidentifying faces in security systems to providing skewed loan approvals. To avoid these pitfalls, AI systems need robust, diverse data sets. Think of it as providing a balanced diet for your AI, ensuring it operates fairly and accurately across all scenarios.

Successful AI adoption doesn't happen by accident; it requires a strategic approach. Comprehensive training programs for AI users are essential. Picture these like driving lessons for the digital age, ensuring users understand how to operate AI systems safely and effectively. Collaboration between AI developers and end-users is also crucial. When developers and users communicate, they ensure the technology meets real-world needs, much like a tailor adjusting a suit for the perfect fit. This collaboration helps developers refine AI solutions, making them more user-friendly and applicable to everyday problems.

History offers us a treasure trove of lessons from AI projects that stumbled. Take, for instance, an AI initiative that underestimated ethical considerations. Perhaps it was designed to streamline hiring processes but ended up discriminating against certain applicants due to biased training data. Such missteps highlight the importance of integrating ethical checks at every stage, ensuring AI systems uphold fairness and equality. Or consider an AI-driven customer service solution that failed spectacularly, frustrating customers with its robotic responses. The takeaway here is clear: AI must enhance the customer experience, not detract from it.

The AI landscape is a dynamic one, and continuous learning is vital to staying ahead. Professional development opportunities in AI are like fuel for your car, keeping you moving forward in your career. Workshops, seminars, and online courses ensure you're up-to-date with the latest advancements, much like a gardener tending to a growing plant. Communities of practice provide another avenue for growth. These groups allow AI enthusiasts to share insights, challenges, and successes, fostering a culture of collaboration and innovation. It's like joining a book club, but instead of discussing novels, you're exploring the latest AI trends and technologies.

As we wrap up this chapter, remember that AI is a powerful tool with immense potential, but like all tools, it requires skillful handling. By learning from past mistakes and embracing a culture of continuous learning, we can navigate the AI landscape with confidence and competence. In the next chapter, we'll explore the exciting fusion of AI with human creativity, where technology meets imagination in ways that are reshaping industries and inspiring new forms of expression.

Chapter Fourteen

AI in Creativity and the Arts

E ver felt like technology is a high-speed train, and you're just hoping to catch a seat? Well, fear not, because this chapter is your express ticket to AI confidence. We're diving into the world of practical AI exercises, where even the most technophobic among us can feel like a digital maestro. So, grab your metaphorical conductor's baton and prepare to orchestrate your first symphony of smart technology. From virtual assistants that rival the most efficient personal secretaries to AI-generated playlists that just seem to get you, it's time to roll up your sleeves and introduce these digital wonders to your everyday life.

Let's start with setting up a virtual assistant. Think of this as your new best friend—one that never forgets birthdays and always knows when to remind you to pick up the dry cleaning. Whether you're using Siri, Alexa, or Google Assistant, the setup is as easy as pie. Simply download the app, follow the guided instructions, and you'll soon have a helper who can manage your calendar, control your smart home devices, or even tell you the weather before you step out the door.

It's like having a personal concierge who never takes a day off. And if you're feeling adventurous, experiment with creating AI-generated playlists. Imagine a DJ who knows your music taste better than you do. Platforms like Spotify use AI to curate playlists based on what you've listened to before, introducing you to new tunes that hit all the right notes.

Once you've got the basics down, it's time to dive into something a bit more complex. How about creating a simple chatbot with pre-defined responses? Picture a digital parrot that echoes your words but with a bit more sophistication. Using platforms like Chatbot.com, you can set up a basic bot that responds to common queries—perfect for small businesses or even personal projects. It's a fun way to dip your toes into the world of AI programming without needing a degree in computer science. And for those with a curious mind, try using AI for basic image recognition tasks. Platforms like Clarifai offer tools that can help you train an AI to recognize objects in photos. It's like teaching a toddler to identify shapes, but without the sticky fingers.

Encouragement is the name of the game when it comes to exploring AI tools. Customize AI recommendations based on your personal interests, whether that's finding the perfect book to read next or discovering a new recipe to try. The more you interact with these tools, the better they understand your preferences, offering suggestions that are as unique as your thumbprint. And don't forget the power of voice commands with smart devices. It's like living in a sci-fi movie where you can control your environment with just your voice. Whether it's dimming the lights, setting the thermostat, or starting a playlist, voice commands make life a little bit more futuristic and a lot more convenient.

Learning is always more fun with friends, so why not form AI study groups or discussion forums? It's like a book club, but instead of novels, you're exploring the latest AI innovations. Share your experiences, compare notes, and maybe even solve a few tech puzzles together. If you prefer a more hands-on approach, consider sharing AI-generated content with friends for feedback. Whether it's a chatbot response or a curated playlist, getting input from others can provide new insights and ideas. Who knows, you might even inspire someone else to take their first steps into the fascinating world of AI.

Reflection Section: Try It Out!

Take a moment to reflect on your AI journey so far. What tools have you tried? What surprised you the most? Write down your thoughts and consider setting a goal for your next AI adventure. Whether it's mastering voice commands or creating a more complex chatbot, each step is a building block in your digital toolkit. Remember, the more you engage with AI, the more intuitive it becomes.

Practical Prompts: Getting the Most Out of ChatGPT

Picture this: you're staring at a blank page, the cursor blinking at you like a digital metronome, and your brain feels like it's running on a half-empty tank of creativity. Enter ChatGPT, your new writing buddy, ready to jumpstart those creative juices and fill that page with brilliance. When using ChatGPT for text generation, the key is crafting effective prompts. Think of it like giving instructions to a very eager, albeit slightly robotic, intern. For instance, if you're in the mood to write a short story, why not prompt ChatGPT with something intriguing like, "Write a plot about a time-traveling librarian who discovers a future where books are banned." Watch as your virtual assistant spins a tale that might just rival your favorite sci-fi thriller. ChatGPT isn't just for the fantastical, though. It's equally at home helping you craft personalized emails and messages. Need to send a heartfelt note to a friend or a professional email to a client? Provide ChatGPT with the right context and tone, and it'll help you draft something that strikes just the right chord.

Now, prompts aren't a one-size-fits-all affair. You may find yourself needing to fine-tune them to hit the mark. It's a bit like seasoning soup: a pinch more here, a dash less there. Adjusting the tone and style in ChatGPT responses can be as simple as adding a few descriptive words to your initial prompt. Want something humorous? Try starting with, "Write in a light-hearted manner," and see how the tone shifts. Experimenting with prompt length and specificity can also yield wonderfully diverse responses. A short prompt like "Write a poem about winter" might get you a haiku, while a more detailed one, "Write a nostalgic poem about the quiet beauty of a snowy evening," could produce a more elaborate ode. Each adjustment in your prompt is like tuning an instrument, finding the right pitch until everything sounds just right.

But ChatGPT isn't merely a tool for writers. Its versatility spans across various applications, proving to be a handy assistant in brainstorming business ideas or shaping marketing strategies. Imagine you're tasked with developing a new campaign for your business. A prompt like, "Generate a list of creative marketing strategies for a sustainable clothing brand," can open up a world of possibilities. Similarly, when you're stuck with writer's block on an academic paper, ChatGPT can help whip up an outline that organizes your thoughts and points you in the right direction. Think of it as having a brainstorming partner who's always ready to throw out ideas, regardless of the time of day.

However, with great power comes great responsibility, and that applies to AI-generated content, too. Promoting ethical use of ChatGPT is crucial. When incorporating AI-assisted writing into your work, always ensure your content remains original. Use the suggestions as a stepping stone, not a crutch. Acknowledge AI contributions in collaborative projects, much like you would credit a co-author. This transparency not only respects the technology but also maintains the integrity of your work. By understanding and respecting these guidelines, you can utilize ChatGPT's capabilities to create content that is both innovative and responsible.

Design Challenges: Creating with Canva and Dall-e

Imagine stepping into a world where creativity dances freely, unhindered by the constraints of traditional design tools. Canva and Dall-e are like your personal creative playgrounds, ready to transform your ideas into stunning visuals. Let's start with Canva, the Swiss Army knife of graphic design. It offers a treasure trove of templates, perfect for designing a social media campaign that pops. Picture this: you're tasked with boosting your presence on Instagram. With Canva, you can craft eye-catching posts and stories that not only grab attention but also tell a compelling brand story. The intuitive drag-and-drop interface makes it feel like play rather than work, as you experiment with layouts, fonts, and images until you find the perfect combination that screams "Look at me!"

Now, turn your gaze to Dall-e, the digital artist who never tires. This tool is your go-to for creating unique artworks inspired by any theme your heart desires. Imagine conjuring an artwork titled "Serenity in Chaos"—a visual juxtaposition that begs for exploration. Input your theme, and watch Dall-e generate art that captures the essence of your imagination. It's like having a genie in a bottle, ready to bring your creative whims to life with a simple text prompt. Whether you're designing for fun or creating a masterpiece for your living room wall, Dall-e is your artistic ally, ready to color outside the lines.

Iteration is the secret sauce of skill-building in design. Imagine being a chef, continuously tasting and tweaking your dish until it reaches perfection. In design, this means testing different color schemes and layouts, allowing your work to evolve through trial and error. Feedback is your best friend in this process. It's like having a taste tester who offers constructive criticism to refine your creation. Seek input from friends, colleagues, or online communities to improve your designs. Each piece of feedback is a breadcrumb on your path to creating something that resonates with your audience.

Storytelling is at the heart of any great design, and with Canva and Dall-e, you can craft visual narratives that captivate and inspire. Consider creating a visual storyboard for a short film. It's like directing a movie scene by scene, using images to convey emotion and plot. Or perhaps you're more inclined toward the world of graphic novels. Use AI-generated art to design a page that captures the tension and drama of your storyline. Each panel is a window into your tale, woven together to form a tapestry of intrigue and excitement.

Collaboration is where creativity truly shines. Picture hosting a virtual design workshop with peers, where ideas flow like a river, each contribution adding depth and richness. Use AI tools to facilitate this collective creativity, allowing participants to build on each other's ideas. It's like a potluck dinner where everyone brings their favorite dish, creating a feast of innovation and inspiration. Alternatively, consider participating in online design challenges or competitions. These events are like the Olympics of creativity, pushing you to explore new techniques and styles while connecting with a community of like-minded enthusiasts.

Inventive Ideograms: Visual Creativity Practice

Imagine a world where pictures speak louder than words, where a single symbol can convey a story deeper than a thousand-page novel. Welcome to the realm of ideograms, where creativity knows no bounds, and expression is as limitless as your imagination. Let's start by designing personal logos or symbols. Think of this as crafting your own signature in the world of art. Whether it's a simple line drawing representing your love for coffee or an intricate emblem capturing the essence of your family heritage, personal logos are a canvas for your identity. They're like the visual equivalent of a catchy theme song, instantly recognizable and uniquely yours. Dive into creating ideograms that represent abstract concepts, like peace, freedom, or even your Monday morning mood. It's a bit like trying to capture the wind in a bottle, challenging yet incredibly rewarding.

Once you've dipped your toes into the pool of ideogram creation, it's time to explore the vast ocean of visual styles. Picture yourself as an adventurous artist, blending traditional techniques with digital prowess to create something truly unique. Experiment with combining the graceful elegance of classical art forms with the crisp precision of digital design. This fusion of old and new can lead to pieces that are both timeless and cutting-edge. Don't shy away from exploring cultural influences in your designs. Draw inspiration from the vibrant patterns of African textiles, the delicate brushstrokes of Japanese calligraphy, or the bold colors of Latin American murals. Each style adds a new layer to your work, enriching it with diversity and depth.

Storytelling through ideograms offers a unique way to convey narratives, allowing viewers to interpret and engage with your work on multiple levels. Imagine developing a visual narrative using a series of ideograms. Each symbol acts as a chapter, contributing to a story that unfolds without a single written word. It could be the tale of a hero's journey, a love story told through intertwined hearts, or even an abstract representation of life's many twists and turns. Crafting a visual poem with symbolic imagery takes this concept a step further, merging art and poetry into a seamless expression of thought and emotion. These visual poems invite viewers to ponder and interpret meaning, creating a dialogue between artist and audience that transcends language barriers.

The beauty of ideograms lies in their versatility, extending beyond art galleries and into various fields like design and education. In the classroom, ideograms can transform complex topics into engaging, memorable lessons. Imagine incorporating them into educational materials to help students grasp abstract concepts like photosynthesis or historical events. These visual representations simplify information, making learning both accessible and enjoyable. In branding and marketing, ideograms are powerful tools for conveying a brand's message at a glance. They serve as visual ambassadors, encapsulating the essence of a product or service in a way that resonates with consumers. A well-designed ideogram can become synonymous with a brand, fostering recognition and loyalty.

As you explore the world of ideograms, remember that creativity thrives on experimentation and exploration. Don't be afraid to push boundaries, try new techniques, and discover your own unique style. Whether you're creating for personal expression or professional purposes, ideograms offer a limitless playground for your imagination. So grab your digital stylus or traditional brush, and let your creativity flow, crafting symbols that speak volumes and inspire those who see them.

AI in Action: Real-World Problem Solving

Imagine waking up in the morning, sipping your coffee, and predicting the day's weather like a seasoned meteorologist. No magic needed, just a simple AI model that you've developed, capable of forecasting local weather patterns. It's like having a miniature weather station right in your living room, offering insights that could help you decide between grabbing an umbrella or opting for sunglasses. Creating such a model doesn't require a degree in meteorology. Platforms like IBM Watson provide user-friendly tools that allow you to input historical weather data and generate forecasts. It's a bit like baking a cake—follow the recipe, adjust as needed, and soon you'll have a model that serves up weather predictions as reliably as your morning toast.

But let's not stop at weather. AI has the potential to revolutionize your approach to health and fitness, offering personalized recommendations that are as unique as your fingerprint. Imagine using AI to craft a fitness plan that not only aligns with your health goals but adapts as you progress. Tools like MyFitnessPal leverage AI to analyze your dietary habits and exercise routines, providing suggestions that keep you on track. It's like having a personal trainer who never tires, always ready to provide the motivation and guidance you need to reach your wellness milestones. Whether you're training for a marathon or simply striving for a healthier lifestyle, AI is your steadfast ally, ensuring your efforts are as effective as possible.

Communities too can benefit from AI-driven solutions, transforming local initiatives with the power of technology. Picture a neighborhood where resources are shared seamlessly, facilitated by an AI-driven platform that connects neighbors in need with those who have surplus. It's like a digital marketplace, but instead of buying and selling, it's about giving and receiving. Whether it's sharing tools, offering a ride, or exchanging homegrown produce, AI fosters a sense of community and cooperation that strengthens neighborhood bonds. Participating in community hackathons focused on AI solutions is another way to contribute. These events are akin to digital barn-raisings, where individuals come together to brainstorm and develop creative solutions to local challenges. It's a chance to flex your mental muscles, collaborate with like-minded individuals, and create something that benefits the greater good.

Innovation thrives when curiosity meets opportunity, and AI experiments are the perfect playground for this marriage. Consider designing a smart home system with customized AI features, turning your living space into a hub of efficiency and comfort. Imagine lights that adjust to your mood, a thermostat that learns your schedule, and appliances that communicate with each other to optimize energy use. It's like having a personal butler who anticipates your needs before you even voice them. Similarly, exploring AI-driven solutions for environmental sustainability can lead to groundbreaking advancements. From AI algorithms that optimize recycling processes to models that predict and mitigate environmental impacts, the possibilities are as vast as they are exciting. Each experiment is a step toward a future where technology and sustainability walk hand in hand, paving the way for a greener, smarter world.

Collaboration is the engine that drives innovation, and AI projects offer fertile ground for partnerships. Joining online AI development communities is like entering a bustling marketplace of ideas, where experts and novices alike share knowledge, offer feedback, and inspire one another. It's a space where your questions lead to answers and your ideas spark new possibilities. Partnering with local businesses for AI innovation projects is another avenue to explore. Whether it's developing AI tools for customer engagement, optimizing supply chain logistics, or enhancing product offerings, these collaborations can lead to mutually beneficial outcomes. It's a win-win, where businesses gain innovative solutions and you gain experience and insights that could shape your future endeavors.

As we wrap up our exploration of AI in action, consider the myriad ways these tools can solve real-world problems, fostering innovation and collaboration in everyday life. In the next chapter, we'll delve into the ethical and social implications of AI, examining the responsibilities and considerations that come with wielding such powerful technology.

Chapter Fifteen

Case Studies: AI Transformations in Everyday Life

P icture yourself strolling through your neighborhood, where the local bakery has suddenly become the talk of the town, not because they've discovered a new type of croissant, but because they've embraced artificial intelligence to turn dough into dough. That's right, folks—AI is now the secret ingredient in small business success. In this chapter, we're diving headfirst into the world of small businesses that have embraced AI as their trusty sidekick. Think of it as Batman and Robin, except with fewer capes and more data analysis.

Small businesses have long been the backbone of our communities, but with AI, they're also becoming the brain. Take customer feedback, for example. Gone are the days when a suggestion box gathered dust in the corner. Now, AI-driven customer feedback analysis is the name of the game, collecting and interpreting data faster than you can say "customer satisfaction." This technology doesn't just gather opinions;

it distills them into actionable insights, helping businesses tweak their services to better meet the needs of their clientele. Imagine a bakery that knows you prefer your baguette with a little more crunch or your donut with a dash of cinnamon, all without you saying a word. It's like having a personal psychic, minus the crystal ball and incense.

And let's not forget the magic of inventory management. Automation in this area has small business owners sleeping soundly at night, knowing their shelves are neither overflowing nor barren. AI helps predict inventory needs with the precision of a seasoned stock market analyst, saving businesses from the dreaded "Sorry, we're out of stock" sign. It's as if a friendly robot is whispering in the ear of the store manager, ensuring they never run out of your favorite artisanal bread. For business owners, it's like having a personal assistant who's never had a bad day or called in sick.

But the wonders of AI don't stop there. It's also a powerful tool for market expansion. Small businesses are using AI in digital marketing strategies that would make Mad Men blush with envy. By analyzing consumer behavior and predicting trends, these businesses can target their ads more effectively, reaching potential customers who didn't even know they needed a new succulent or a hand-knit scarf. It's like having a marketing guru in your pocket, who knows exactly when and where to place that perfect ad. And in the world of online shopping, personalization is key. AI allows small businesses to tailor shopping experiences to individual preferences, turning casual browsers into loyal customers. It's like having a personal stylist who understands your taste better than you do.

Moreover, AI is helping small businesses trim the fat, so to speak, reducing operational costs and improving efficiency. Streamlined supply chain management, powered by AI, ensures that products move from point A to point B with the grace of a prima ballerina. This is not just about saving money; it's about making every dollar count. And by automating routine tasks, businesses can reduce labor costs, freeing up employees to focus on more complex, value-added activities. It's like having a team of invisible helpers, working tirelessly in the background to keep the wheels turning smoothly.

Consider the case of a local bakery, which might sound like a humble establishment, but with AI, it's anything but ordinary. By using AI for inventory prediction, this bakery ensures that every croissant and baguette is fresh, delicious, and never wasted. It's a balancing act worthy of a trapeze artist, ensuring they bake just enough to satisfy demand without overfilling their display cases. Or take a boutique clothing store, which employs AI for trend analysis, staying ahead of fashion curves and ensuring their racks are filled with what's hot and new. By analyzing fashion trends and consumer preferences, they keep their stock as stylish as their clientele. These aren't just success stories; they're transformations, showcasing how AI can turn small businesses into local legends.

Reflection Section: Consider Your Business

Think about your own business or a small business you admire. How could AI help improve operations, customer service, or marketing? Reflect on potential areas where AI can be integrated to enhance efficiency and customer experience.

These case studies highlight the transformative power of AI in small business landscapes, where innovation meets tradition, and where technology fuels growth and creativity. AI isn't just a tool; it's a catalyst for change, helping small businesses flourish in ways they never imagined possible.

Family Dynamics: AI in Everyday Parenting

Imagine waking up to a household where chaos has taken a back-seat. The morning rush, which once resembled a scene from a dis-aster movie, is now a well-orchestrated ballet of efficiency. Thanks to AI-powered family calendars, managing schedules has never been easier. These digital lifesavers sync effortlessly across all family members, ensuring everyone knows when ballet lessons, soccer practice, and the infamous dentist appointments are happening. It's like having a personal assistant for each family member, minus the hefty paycheck. With real-time updates, nobody misses a beat—no more frantic calls asking if it's your turn to pick up the kids. You can even find apps that suggest the best times for family dinners or movie nights, ensuring quality time remains a priority amidst the hustle and bustle of daily life.

Now, let's talk about smart home devices, the unsung heroes of daily routines. These gadgets have a knack for turning your home into a futuristic oasis of calm and order. Imagine a scenario where your coffee brews itself while your curtains open gently to let in the morning sun. It sounds like science fiction, but it's the reality with smart home integration. From setting reminders to managing chores, these devices are like having a mini butler who never takes a day off. They can adjust lighting and temperature based on your preferences, ensuring your home is always comfortable and inviting. It's as if your house finally understands you, responding to your needs with the efficiency of a seasoned concierge.

When it comes to child development, AI is making significant strides. Educational apps tailored for children are turning learning into an adventure, engaging young minds with interactive content that's both fun and informative. These apps adapt to each child's

learning pace, offering personalized challenges that keep them motivated without overwhelming them. It's like having a teacher who
knows exactly when to push and when to pause, ensuring no child is
left behind. And then there's interactive storytelling, where AI weaves
tales that captivate imaginations, turning bedtime stories into immersive experiences. Kids can choose characters, alter storylines, and even
interact with the narrative, making every story as unique as they are.

Parental concerns about safety in the digital age are not to be taken
lightly, and AI steps up to this challenge with aplomb. AI monitoring
tools provide parents with peace of mind, keeping a watchful eye on
their children's online activities. These tools alert parents to potential
hazards, ensuring kids can explore the digital world safely. It's like
having a digital guardian angel, always vigilant and ready to intervene
if things go awry. Smart home security systems add another layer of
safety, with features like cameras and sensors that ensure your home
is as secure as a fortress. Whether you're home or away, these systems
provide real-time updates, allowing you to monitor your space and
respond to any issues promptly.

Let's hear from a family who has embraced AI in their daily lives.
Meet the Johnsons, a bustling household with three kids, two jobs,
and one very energetic dog. They've integrated AI tools to streamline
meal planning and nutrition, using apps that suggest recipes based
on their dietary preferences and automatically generate shopping lists.
No more "What's for dinner?" panic at the end of a long day. With AI,
the Johnsons enjoy healthy, varied meals that cater to everyone's tastes.
They've also leveraged AI to manage extracurricular activities, ensuring every soccer game, piano lesson, and scout meeting is accounted
for, without the usual scheduling headaches.

For parents juggling multiple responsibilities, AI offers a lifeline,
transforming household management from a constant struggle into a

seamless operation. It's about enhancing family dynamics, giving you time back to focus on what truly matters—spending quality moments with your loved ones. Whether it's coordinating schedules, ensuring your children's safety, or simply making everyday tasks more manageable, AI is there, redefining the modern family experience with a touch of technology and a dash of magic.

Community Engagement: AI in Local Initiatives

Imagine walking down Main Street and seeing your local government offices bustling with efficiency. AI has stepped into local government services like a superhero in a suit and tie, handling the mundane tasks that used to bog down public servants. From managing city resources to optimizing public safety, AI is the quiet partner that makes everything run smoother. Think of it as the equivalent of a digital Swiss Army knife, ready to tackle any issue from traffic congestion to permit applications with ease. By analyzing data faster than a speeding bullet, AI tools help city planners make informed decisions, leading to better services for everyone. It's not about replacing the hardworking people behind the scenes but supporting them to focus on what truly matters—serving the community.

In the realm of community health initiatives, AI shines even brighter. Picture a scenario where instead of long waits and cumbersome paperwork, your local clinic uses AI to streamline processes, from patient intake to diagnostics. AI can predict health trends within the community, allowing clinics to prepare for flu seasons or outbreaks with the precision of a seasoned meteorologist predicting a storm. It's like having a personal health assistant who knows the medical history of an entire community and can suggest preventive measures accordingly. These tools not only improve efficiency but also enhance the quality of care received, making health services more responsive and accessible to everyone.

Switching gears to environmental sustainability, AI is the unsung hero in waste management and recycling. Imagine a world where waste is sorted more efficiently than your sock drawer, thanks to AI-driven sorting systems. These systems use machine learning to identify and separate materials, ensuring that recycling programs are as effective as they can be. In addition, smart city technologies are more than just buzzwords; they're tangible solutions that improve energy efficiency. By managing resources intelligently, AI reduces wastage, turning cities into lean, green machines. From smart lighting systems that adjust based on daylight to water management solutions that prevent leaks, AI is making sustainable living not just possible but practical.

Communities have also embraced AI to tackle local challenges with flair and innovation. Public transportation systems are a prime example, where AI optimizes routes and schedules to reduce wait times and improve commuter experiences. Imagine a bus system that knows when you're running late and adjusts its schedule to accommodate, all while reducing fuel consumption and emissions. Community education programs, too, are leveraging AI tools to provide personalized learning experiences, ensuring that education is tailored to meet the needs of every learner. Whether it's language learning or vocational training, AI enhances accessibility and engagement, offering resources that adapt to varied learning styles.

Take the example of an urban neighborhood employing AI for crime prediction. By analyzing patterns and trends, AI can help law enforcement anticipate criminal activity and allocate resources more effectively. It's like having a crystal ball that sees into the future, allowing police to prevent incidents before they happen. This proactive approach not only boosts community safety but also builds trust between residents and law enforcement. In rural areas, AI plays a pivotal role in agricultural improvement. Farmers use AI to predict weather patterns, optimize planting schedules, and even manage livestock health. It's as if they have a digital farmhand, offering insights that maximize yield and sustainability.

These examples illustrate how AI is more than just a technological advancement; it's a catalyst for community development and empowerment. By integrating AI into local initiatives, communities can address challenges with renewed vigor and creativity, ensuring they thrive in an ever-changing world.

Creative Ventures: Artists and AI Collaboration

Imagine standing in an art gallery where the walls vibrate with colors and forms that seem to defy the imagination. You might wonder, "Who could dream up such intricate patterns and mind-bending visuals?" The answer, my dear reader, is a collaboration between artists and artificial intelligence. In recent years, AI has waltzed into the art world, offering creative souls new ways to express their visions. Artists are now using generative art algorithms to push the boundaries of their work, producing pieces that are as unpredictable as they are beautiful. These algorithms act like digital paintbrushes, capable of creating complex patterns and textures that would take a human artist weeks, if not months, to achieve. Imagine a canvas that evolves in real-time, reacting to every brushstroke with a burst of creativity that feels almost alive.

But AI isn't just making waves in the visual arts; it's also composing symphonies in concert halls. Music composition and sound design have become fertile grounds for AI's creative prowess. Picture AI as a collaborator in the studio, suggesting melodies and harmonies that

challenge traditional notions of music. AI analyzes existing compositions and draws inspiration from them, crafting new pieces that blend
genres in ways that surprise and delight. It's like having a co-composer
who's always in tune with what your music needs, whether it's a
haunting melody or a foot-tapping rhythm. This partnership between
human and machine results in soundscapes that are as rich and varied
as the artists themselves.

The art world is also witnessing an explosion of collaborative projects where AI plays a starring role. Take, for instance, AI-assisted
installations and performances, where technology and creativity meet
on stage. Artists are using AI to create dynamic environments that
respond to audience interaction, transforming spectators into participants in the artistic process. Imagine a performance where the backdrop shifts and morphs in response to the performers' movements,
creating a living, breathing piece of art. These collaborations extend to
exhibitions featuring AI-generated art, where traditional boundaries
are blurred, and visitors are invited to explore art that's as innovative
as it is immersive.

AI's impact on creative industries doesn't stop at galleries and concert halls. It's also reshaping film and animation production, offering
filmmakers new tools to bring their stories to life. AI can transform
a script into a visual spectacle, providing directors with digital effects
that would make even the most seasoned CGI artists envious. In fashion, AI is sparking innovation by predicting trends and suggesting
designs that push the envelope. Imagine a world where your wardrobe
is curated by an intelligent assistant that knows your style better than
you do, creating garments that are both cutting-edge and timeless.

Let's take a deeper look at some artists who have embraced AI in
their work, creating masterpieces that capture the imagination. Consider a visual artist who uses AI to design digital sculptures, each piece

a testament to the fusion of human creativity and machine precision. These sculptures challenge our perception of art, offering forms and structures that are as thought-provoking as they are beautiful. Or a music producer who employs AI to craft unique soundscapes, blending traditional instruments with digital ones to create compositions that transcend genres. This producer isn't just making music; they're crafting experiences that resonate on a deeply emotional level.

In this chapter, we've explored how AI is transforming the landscape of creativity, breaking down barriers and opening new avenues for expression. Artists and AI are collaborating in ways that redefine what it means to create, blending the old with the new in a dance as graceful as it is revolutionary. As we move forward, consider the potential of AI to not just enhance our creative endeavors but to redefine them altogether. Next, we'll explore the broader implications of AI in the workplace and how it's shaping the future of productivity.

Chapter Sixteen

Practical AI Applications for Daily Life

I magine for a moment that you're at the helm of a spaceship, ready to explore the uncharted territories of the future, where AI is the co-pilot guiding you through galaxies of possibilities. Sounds thrilling, right? In this chapter, we'll embark on a voyage to uncover the newest and most exciting frontiers of AI innovation. We'll peek into the world of quantum computing, where computers use qubits—imagine them as supercharged light bulbs that can be both on and off at the same time—to tackle problems faster than a kid solving a Rubik's Cube. Quantum computing and AI together promise to transform everything from healthcare to autonomous vehicles, where cars don't just drive themselves but do so while planning the best route to your favorite coffee shop. The future is not just about faster machines; it's about smarter solutions that anticipate our needs, sometimes before we even know we have them.

Emerging fields are also ripe for AI's touch. Enter synthetic biology, where AI helps design and optimize genetic sequences, paving the way for synthetic organisms that could one day produce environmentally friendly fuels or even glow-in-the-dark plants for your garden. The possibilities are endless, with AI predicting protein structures more accurately than your local weather forecast. Imagine AI-driven drug discovery platforms revolutionizing medicine by identifying novel compounds faster than a chef whipping up a new recipe. By integrating AI into these fields, we're not just advancing technology; we're redefining the boundaries of science and innovation. It's like having an army of tiny, invisible scientists working around the clock to solve the world's biggest puzzles.

AI's influence doesn't stop there. It's driving the convergence of technologies, where once separate worlds now collide to create something greater than the sum of their parts. Take the Internet of Things (IoT) as an example, where your fridge, toaster, and even your doorbell are part of a vast network, all talking to each other in a digital symphony. AI orchestrates this concert, ensuring everything works in harmony, like a conductor leading a world-class orchestra. Add blockchain into the mix, and you've got a recipe for enhanced security, where data is as safe as Fort Knox, and transactions are transparent and tamper-proof. This convergence is more than just a trend; it's the dawn of a new era where technology doesn't just serve us but elevates our daily lives.

And what about the final frontier? Yes, space. AI is set to play a starring role in space exploration, guiding probes to distant planets and sifting through cosmic data to find habitable worlds. Imagine AI-enhanced virtual reality experiences that take you on a tour of Mars from the comfort of your living room, no space suit required. It's the stuff of sci-fi dreams, but it's becoming our reality. AI doesn't just stop at improving what we know; it expands the horizons of what we dream. It's like opening a book and finding an entirely new chapter you never knew existed.

Reflection Section: Future AI Innovations

Consider the impact AI could have on your daily life. How might these emerging technologies change your routines, from your morning coffee to your evening entertainment? Reflect on how AI's role in the future could transform the way we live, work, and connect with the world around us. What excites you the most about these possibilities? Take a moment to jot down your thoughts, and perhaps share them with a friend or family member. After all, the future is a conversation we're all part of, and your ideas might just be the spark that lights the way forward.

AI and Sustainability: Innovations for a Better World

Picture this: a world where AI not only helps you find the fastest route to work but also plays a superhero role in saving the planet. In the realm of environmental protection, AI is making waves that even the most seasoned surfer would envy. Take wildlife conservation, for instance. AI-driven monitoring systems are like vigilant park rangers, tirelessly tracking animal movements and alerting conservationists to potential threats. These systems use drones and camera traps to gather data, identifying endangered species and helping protect their habitats. Imagine an AI-powered sidekick that never sleeps, always on the lookout to ensure our wildlife thrives, from the tiniest insects to the mighty elephants.

But AI's eco-friendly efforts don't stop there. Sustainable agriculture has become a reality thanks to AI-driven resource management. Think of AI as the ultimate farmhand, analyzing soil conditions, weather patterns, and crop health to optimize yields and reduce waste. Farmers can now make informed decisions on irrigation and pest control, minimizing chemical use and conserving water. It's like having a crystal ball that predicts the best farming practices, ensuring the land remains fertile for generations. AI is transforming agriculture into a sustainable force, allowing us to feed the world while nurturing the environment.

Switching gears to renewable energy, AI is revolutionizing how we harness nature's power. In solar energy, AI optimizes panel placement and angles, squeezing every last drop of sunshine to boost efficiency. It's as if AI whispers to the sun, coaxing it to shine a little brighter on our behalf. For wind energy, AI analytics predict wind patterns with the precision of a seasoned meteorologist, ensuring turbines spin at optimal speeds. These advancements make renewable energy sources more viable and reliable, paving the way to a greener future. With AI at the helm, renewable energy isn't just a dream—it's the engine driving our sustainable tomorrow.

Waste not, want not, as the old saying goes, and AI is taking this to heart by tackling waste reduction head-on. Imagine AI-powered waste sorting systems that can tell a yogurt cup from a soda can faster than you can say "recycle." These systems use advanced vision technology to sort recyclables accurately, reducing contamination and improving recycling rates. Circular economy models, supported by AI, encourage the reuse and repurposing of materials, minimizing the need for new resources. It's like turning waste into treasure, with AI as the alchemist making it all possible.

When it comes to climate change, AI isn't sitting on the sidelines. Climate modeling and prediction using AI are akin to having an army of supercomputers that can analyze vast amounts of data, providing more accurate forecasts and strategies for mitigation. AI interventions aim to reduce carbon emissions by optimizing energy usage and improving transportation networks. Picture AI as the ultimate eco-warrior, fighting climate change one algorithm at a time.

As AI continues to evolve, its potential to address environmental challenges grows exponentially. Whether it's protecting endangered species or optimizing renewable energy, AI is a powerful ally in our quest for sustainability. It's not just about technology; it's about creating a world where future generations can thrive alongside nature, with AI as the guiding force.

AI in Healthcare: Revolutionizing Medicine

Picture this: a world where going to the doctor is as simple and effective as ordering a pizza online. AI is revolutionizing healthcare, taking diagnostics to levels only dreamt of in sci-fi novels. Imagine walking into a radiology department where AI helps radiologists detect diseases with the precision of a hawk spotting its prey. AI systems can analyze scans and X-rays faster and more accurately than ever before, catching anomalies that might slip past the human eye. This means earlier detection, better treatment plans, and ultimately, more lives saved. And let's not forget AI-driven genetic testing, which deciphers your DNA like a cryptic crossword, identifying genetic predispositions and enabling personalized health strategies. It's like having a fortune teller who actually knows what they're talking about, guiding you toward healthier choices.

AI doesn't stop at diagnostics; it's reshaping patient care, too. Remote patient monitoring systems powered by AI act like digital nurses, keeping tabs on vital signs and alerting healthcare providers to potential issues before they become emergencies. Imagine a watch that not only tells time but also keeps an eye on your heart, sending real-time updates to your doctor. This technology allows for person-alized medicine that goes beyond "one-size-fits-all" to tailor treatment plans based on individual data. It's like having a bespoke suit, but for your health. AI analyzes vast amounts of patient data to recommend personalized treatment paths, optimizing outcomes and minimizing side effects. In this way, AI isn't just a tool; it's a partner in your health journey, working alongside your medical team to ensure you get the best care possible.

On the research front, AI is accelerating medical advancements at a pace that makes traditional methods look like dial-up in an age of fiber optics. AI systems are instrumental in drug repurposing and develop-ment, identifying new uses for existing drugs faster than you can say "Eureka!" This speeds up the time it takes to bring treatments from the lab to the pharmacy, offering hope for conditions that previously had limited options. AI also plays a crucial role in analyzing clinical trial data, sifting through mountains of information to identify patterns and insights that might otherwise go unnoticed. It's like having a de-tective on the case, ensuring no clue is left unturned. These advance-ments mean more effective treatments and, by extension, healthier populations.

Looking to the future, AI's potential in healthcare stretches as wide as the horizon. Consider robotic surgery, where AI assists surgeons with precision that rivals the steadiest of hands. Imagine robots ex-ecuting complex procedures with the guidance of AI, reducing the margin for error and enhancing recovery times. But with great power comes great responsibility. Ethical considerations loom large, partic-ularly around privacy and security in AI-powered medical devices. Ensuring patient data remains confidential and secure is paramount, akin to guarding a treasure chest. As we integrate these technologies into healthcare, the challenge will be balancing innovation with ethical stewardship, ensuring AI serves the common good without compromising individual rights.

In this brave new world, AI is not just a futuristic concept; it's a present-day reality transforming healthcare from the ground up. Whether it's through enhancing diagnostic accuracy, personalizing patient care, or accelerating medical research, AI is the catalyst driving these changes. The road ahead is paved with potential, promising a future where healthcare is more efficient, accessible, and effective than ever before.

AI and Education: Transforming Learning Environments

Imagine a classroom where every student feels like the teacher's favorite. Not because they're the apple-polisher, but because AI tailors the learning experience to fit each student's unique needs. AI in personalized education is like a bespoke tailor for the mind, crafting educational experiences that are as individual as a snowflake. Adaptive learning platforms are the new classroom aides, adjusting content in real-time based on a student's performance. If little Johnny aces fractions but struggles with decimals, AI steps in to offer extra practice, like a digital tutor who never complains about overtime. This isn't just about improving grades; it's about building confidence and nurturing a lifelong love for learning.

Teachers aren't left out in the cold, either. AI-enhanced teaching tools are revolutionizing the way educators approach their craft. Think of AI as the trusty sidekick to every superhero teacher, helping create dynamic learning environments where boredom is banished. AI-driven content creation simplifies lesson planning, generating engaging material that captivates even the most distracted of students. Virtual teaching assistants, powered by AI, handle routine tasks like grading, giving teachers more time to focus on what really matters—igniting the spark of curiosity in their pupils. Imagine a classroom where technology doesn't replace teachers but empowers them to be even more impactful.

Now, picture a world where educational access and equity are more than just buzzwords. AI is breaking down barriers, ensuring that learning is accessible to all, regardless of language or ability. In multilingual classrooms, AI language translation tools are the unsung heroes, translating lessons in real-time and ensuring that no student is left behind because of a language barrier. Meanwhile, AI tools for special education support create inclusive environments where every student can thrive. These tools adapt to different learning needs, providing personalized support that empowers students with disabilities to succeed alongside their peers. It's like having an educational Swiss Army knife, ready to tackle any challenge that comes its way.

As we look to the future, the possibilities for AI-driven educational models are as vast as the imagination. Imagine immersive learning experiences where students can explore ancient civilizations through virtual reality, walking through the streets of Rome or climbing the pyramids of Egypt without leaving their desks. AI-powered global classrooms could connect students from different continents, fostering cross-cultural understanding and collaboration. Picture a science class where students conduct virtual experiments with peers from around the world, sharing insights and discoveries in real-time. This isn't just about technology; it's about creating a global community of learners who are curious, engaged, and ready to tackle the challenges of tomorrow.

Education is evolving, and AI is at the forefront of this transformation. The traditional classroom is giving way to a more interactive, inclusive, and personalized learning environment. In this brave new world, students aren't just passive recipients of information; they're active participants in their own education, guided by technology that's as adaptable as it is intelligent. With AI, the future of education is bright, promising a world where every student has the opportunity to succeed, regardless of where they start.

Preparing for Tomorrow: AI Skills for the Future

Think of entering an AI-driven job market as stepping into a bustling bazaar where everyone's trading in data and innovation. In this vibrant marketplace, being able to analyze and interpret data is like having the hottest commodity around. These skills let you sift through mountains of information to find the nuggets of wisdom hidden within. It's like being a digital detective, piecing together clues to unveil insights that can drive decisions, whether you're in marketing, healthcare, or even agriculture. With data as the new oil, those who can refine it into actionable insights will find themselves in high demand, wielding knowledge like a superpower.

But let's not overlook the softer side of AI—ethics and governance. Understanding these aspects is akin to knowing the rules of a board game where AI is the star player. This knowledge ensures that AI systems are used responsibly, avoiding pitfalls like bias and privacy violations. It's not just about knowing what AI can do but understanding what it should do. Ethical AI use is like being a good neighbor in the digital community, ensuring that the benefits of AI are shared fairly and that the technology doesn't become a bull in a china shop. This balance of technical and ethical skills forms the foundation of thriving in an AI-focused career landscape.

As we march towards an AI-dominated future, continuous education becomes a trusty companion. Online AI courses and certifications are like the treasure maps of the digital world, guiding you to new skills and opportunities. Whether you're a seasoned professional or a curious novice, AI-focused workshops and seminars offer hands-on experience and insights from industry leaders. Imagine them as digital boot camps, where you can flex your mental muscles and come away with new abilities that make you more adaptable and valuable in any field. Lifelong learning in AI is not just a suggestion; it's a necessity in a world where technology evolves faster than the latest fashion trend.

Career opportunities in AI are as diverse as the colors in a painter's palette, with new roles emerging all the time. In creative industries, AI is becoming the muse, aiding in everything from content creation to music composition. Imagine AI as a silent collaborator, offering fresh ideas and providing tools that inspire creativity. In cybersecurity and data protection, AI roles are like the digital guardians, safeguarding information in an era where data breaches are more common than misplaced socks. These roles blend technology with creativity and vigilance, offering career paths that are as rewarding as they are challenging.

To truly thrive in this AI-centric world, proactive engagement is key. Think of joining AI research communities as entering a bustling café filled with lively conversations and idea exchanges. It's a space where you can collaborate, innovate, and contribute to the cutting-edge developments in AI. Open-source AI projects are like collaborative art pieces, where each contributor adds their brushstroke to create something greater than the sum of its parts. By engaging with these communities, you not only enhance your skills but also become part of a collective effort to shape the future of AI. It's about being a participant, not just a spectator, in the AI revolution.

In preparing for tomorrow, we must embrace both the opportunities and responsibilities that AI brings. By honing skills in data analysis and ethics, engaging in continuous education, exploring diverse career paths, and actively participating in AI communities, we're not just preparing for the future—we're helping to build it. As we look ahead, remember that AI is not just a tool but a partner in progress, offering possibilities limited only by our imagination and willingness to learn.

Help Others with Your Review

Make AI Easy for Everyone

"A little help goes a long way." - Anonymous

The best way to learn is by sharing what we know. When we take a moment to help someone else, we make the world a little better—not just for them, but for ourselves too.

So, I have a question for you...

Would you help a stranger if it cost you nothing?

This person is like you—curious about AI, eager to understand it, but maybe not sure where to start. They want to use AI to make life easier, work smarter, and stay ahead in a fast-changing world.

That's why *The AI Handbook for Everyone* exists—to make AI simple, clear, and useful for everyday people. But to reach more readers, we need your help.

A quick review of the book—just a few words about what you liked—can help someone decide to take that first step into AI.

Review Link – https://www.amazon.com/review/create-review/?ie=UTF8&channel=glance-detail&asin=B0DXSH3Y4J

If this book has helped you, inspired you, or made AI a little less confusing, your review can do the same for someone else.

And that's how we grow together.

Thank you for being part of this journey.

Chapter Seventeen

Conclusion

W ell, my dear reader, we've reached the end of our AI adventure, but don't worry—this isn't goodbye. Think of it more like a "see you later" because your journey with artificial intelligence is just beginning. Throughout this book, we've explored the incredible potential of AI tools like Canva, Ideogram, ChatGPT, MidJourney, and Dall-e. We've discovered how these technologies can transform not only your personal life but also the way you work and create.

From the very first chapter, our goal has been to demystify AI and make it accessible to everyone. We've broken down complex concepts into everyday language, using analogies and examples that resonate with your daily life. Whether you're a student, a senior, or an office worker, this book has shown you that AI isn't just for tech wizards—it's for anyone with a curious mind and a willingness to learn.

We've covered a lot of ground together, from the basics of AI to its practical applications in productivity, creativity, and problem-solving. You've learned how to use AI to streamline your schedule, automate tasks, and even predict the weather. We've explored the ways AI can enhance your artistic pursuits, whether you're designing a logo, composing music, or writing a novel. And we've seen how AI can help solve real-world challenges, from improving healthcare to protecting the environment.

But more than just a tool, AI is a catalyst for personal growth and lifelong learning. As you've worked through the exercises and prompts in this book, you've not only gained new skills but also discovered new passions and possibilities. You've become more confident in your ability to navigate the digital landscape and harness the power of technology for your own goals.

So, what's next? The possibilities are endless, but the key is to keep learning and exploring. Stay curious about the world around you and how AI can help you engage with it in new ways. Join online communities, attend workshops, and collaborate with others who share your interests. The future of AI is bright, and by continuing to learn and adapt, you'll be ready to shine right along with it.

As we close this chapter of our journey together, I want to thank you for your trust, your enthusiasm, and your willingness to embrace the unknown. It's been an honor to be your guide through the exciting world of AI, and I hope this book has not only informed you but also inspired you to keep pushing the boundaries of what's possible.

Remember, AI is not about replacing human intelligence but about enhancing it. It's a tool that can help you work smarter, create more freely, and connect more deeply with the world around you. So go forth and experiment, innovate, and most importantly, have fun! The future is yours to shape, and with AI by your side, there's no limit to what you can achieve.

Key Takeaway: AI is not just a technology; it's a partner in your journey of lifelong learning and personal growth. By embracing AI tools and staying curious about their possibilities, you'll be empowered to navigate the digital landscape with confidence and creativity.

The future is bright, and with AI by your side, you have the power to shape it in ways that are uniquely your own.

References

- *I've tested a lot of AI tools for work. These 4 actually help ...* https://www.zdnet.com/article/ive-tested-a-lot-of-ai-tools-for-work-these-4-actually-help-me-get-more-done-every-day/

- *Case Studies: SMEs Successfully Implementing AI Solutions* https://profiletree.com/smes-successfully-implementing-ai-solutions/

- *Debunking AI Myths: The Truth Behind 5 Common ...* https://www.forbes.com/sites/bernardmarr/2023/07/05/debunking-ai-myths-the-truth-behind-5-common-misconceptions/

- *How Artificial Intelligence (AI) Helps Improve Accessibility* https://about.att.com/sites/accessibility/stories/how-ai-helps-accessibility

- *AI Scheduling Assistant: Top 10 Tools for 2024 (Tested)* https://www.meetjamie.ai/blog/ai-scheduling-assistant

- *AI in Smart Homes: Security, Efficiency Automation* https://www.gearbrain.com/ai-smart-home-automati

on-devices-2671168897.html

- *9 AI-Powered Apps That Help You Save Money* https://www.bankrate.com/banking/savings/ai-apps-to-help-you-save-money/

- *How to Use ChatGPT to Meal Plan* - https://percolatekitchen.com/how-to-use-chatgpt-to-meal-plan/

- *How to use Canva AI tools to enhance your designs* https://zapier.com/blog/canva-ai/

- *A beginner's guide to image generation with DALL-E 3* https://medium.com/centerforcooperativemedia/a-beginners-guide-to-image-generation-with-dall-e-3-4efd969ab8fb

- *Midjourney for music - Best AI music generators* https://www.perfectlancer.com/blog/midjourney-for-music%EF%BF%BC

- *Writing with AI* https://openai.com/chatgpt/use-cases/writing-with-ai/

- *8 Top Business Automation Tools to Use in 2023* https://automateddreams.com/blog/8-top-business-automation-tools-to-use-in-2023/

- *How to Use ChatGPT to Write Emails | ClickUp* https://clickup.com/blog/how-to-use-chatgpt-to-write-emails/

- *How AI is revolutionizing Modern Supply Chain Management* https://www.straive.com/blogs/how-ai-is-revolutionizing-modern-supply-chain-management/

- *Case studies: how SMEs are using AI to compete with big ...* https://insidesmallbusiness.com.au/people-hr/productivity/case-studies-how-smes-are-using-ai-to-compete-with-big-players

- *Recommendation on the Ethics of Artificial Intelligence* https://www.unesco.org/en/articles/recommendation-ethics-artificial-intelligence

- *Bias Mitigation Strategies and Techniques for ...* https://www.holisticai.com/blog/bias-mitigation-strategies-techniques-for-classification-tasks

- *Artificial Intelligence (AI) In Cybersecurity* https://www.fortinet.com/resources/cyberglossary/artificial-intelligence-in-cybersecurity

- *Research: How Gen AI Is Already Impacting the Labor Market* https://hbr.org/2024/11/research-how-gen-ai-is-already-impacting-the-labor-market

- *AI-driven adaptive learning for sustainable educational ...* https://onlinelibrary.wiley.com/doi/10.1002/sd.3221#:~:text=Through%20the%20utilization%20of%20intelligent,et%20al.%2C%202023).

- *Best AI Language Learning Apps in 2024 - Heylama* https://www.heylama.com/blog/best-ai-language-learning-apps

- *AI Coaching App | Rocky - Platform for Personal Development* https://www.rocky.ai/

- *Artificial Intelligence and Neuroscience: Transformative ...*

https://www.mdpi.com/2077-0383/14/2/550

- *Case Studies: SMEs Successfully Implementing AI Solutions* https://profiletree.com/smes-successfully-implementing-ai-solutions/

- *Streamlining Family Life with AI: From Homework to Meal ...* https://visitevergladescity.com/streamlining-family-life-with-ai-from-homework-to-meal-planning/

- *Top 50 NGOs Leveraging AI to Drive Social Impact and ...* https://www.linkedin.com/pulse/top-50-ngos-leveraging-ai-drive-social-impact-address-global-challenges-mpanc

- *Creative Collaboration: How Artists and AI Can Work ...* https://medium.com/higher-neurons/creative-collaboration-how-artists-and-ai-can-work-together-187502fd8fdb

- *AI in Elderly Care: Innovative Monitoring and Assistance Tech* https://newo.ai/insights/how-ai-enhances-elderly-care-monitoring-and-assistance-technologies/

- *The 8 best AI scheduling assistants* https://zapier.com/blog/best-ai-scheduling/

- *AI Security: Risks, Frameworks, and Best Practices* https://perception-point.io/guides/ai-security/ai-security-risks-frameworks-and-best-practices/

- *Case Studies: SMEs Successfully Implementing AI Solutions* https://profiletree.com/smes-successfully-implementing-ai-solutions/

- *How to Use ChatGPT for Business* https://elfsight.com/blo
  g/how-to-use-chatgpt-for-business/

- *Getting Started Guide* https://docs.midjourney.com/hc/en
  -us/articles/33329261836941-Getting-Started-Guide

- *11 Social Media Design Tips to Boost Your Visual Strategy* https://www.canva.com/learn/getting-started-social-m
  edia-design/

- *7 examples of real businesses using DALL·E for visual content*
  https://zapier.com/blog/dall-e-examples/#:~:text=Kam%20
  Talebi%2C%20CEO%20of%20Butcher's,wanted%20somet
  hing%20unique%20and%20affordable.

- *Quantum Computing and the Future of AI* https://iot.eeti
  mes.com/quantum-computing-and-the-future-of-ai/

- *Artificial Intelligence Powering Synthetic Biology*
  https://www.spglobal.com/en/research-insights/special-rep
  orts/artificial-intelligence-powering-synthetic-biology-the-f
  undamentals

- *Artificial Intelligence in Renewable Energy* https://www.st
  ax.com/insights/artificial-intelligence-in-renewable-energy

- *The Role of AI in Personalized Learning | Claned*
  https://claned.com/the-role-of-ai-in-personalized-learning/
  #:~:text=1.-,Adaptive%20Learning,customized%2C%20ap
  propriate%20content%20and%20exercises.

Made in the USA
Columbia, SC
11 March 2025

55041341R00113